# Getting it Right with Type

Published in 2006 by Laurence King Publishing Ltd
361-373 City Road
London EC1V 1JJ
United Kingdom
e-mail: enquiries@laurenceking.co.uk
www.laurenceking.co.uk

First published by arrangement with Verlag Hermann Schmidt Mainz
Copyright © 2000 Verlag Hermann Schmidt Mainz
Copyright design © 2006 Laurence King Publishing Ltd

A catalogue record for this book is available from the British Library.

ISBN-13: 978-1-85669-474-2
ISBN-10: 1-85669-474-7

Designed by David Smart
Cover design by Angus Hyland, Pentagram Design Ltd and David Smart
Picture research by Hannah Storey
Printed in Singapore

# Getting it Right with Type

Victoria Squire
Hans Peter Willberg
Friedrich Forssman

Laurence King Publishing

# Contents

## 1

## Typography

Letterforms and typefaces

## 2

## Text

Words and paragraphs

Author's acknowledgements

I wish to thank my colleagues at the University of
Plymouth for all their support and advice whilst writing
this book, in particular Joanne Davies, Stuart Mealing,
Adrian Smith, Peter Jones, David Smart, Lizzie Ridout
and Phil Corby.

I also wish to record my gratitude to all the students
that have enriched and shaped my views over the years
through their thoughts on, and reactions to, type.

*Getting it Right with Type* is based on a German title,
and I would like to thank the authors, Hans Peter
Willberg and Friedrich Forssman whose experience and
writing formed the basis of this book.

I would like to give a special thanks to David Smart,
the designer of this book, for all the advice and
invaluable assistance he has given; Catherine Dixon
and Phil Baines for their assistance in sourcing
imagery; Kirsty and Chris Sarris for their advice on type
from the American perspective; and especially to Jo
Lightfoot, editor at Laurence King, for all her help,
advice and calmness.

I would like to thank my family, Barbara, Rod, Kirsty,
Chris and Sonia who have provided enormous support
and encouragement. In particular, my parents, Barbara
and Rod, whose commitment and tireless work ethic
have been a constant inspiration.

Finally, I have leaned, probably too much, on the
support and goodwill of my husband, Robin, who
has had no choice but to live with this book, and has
walked every step of the way with me. To him, then,
this book is dedicated.

Victoria Squire

# Introduction

'You shouldn't have written this book', was the reaction of a few colleagues from the professional typographic scene. 'If you explain it all to beginners and amateurs, we'll lose all our clients.' I think that just the opposite is true. Do-it-yourself typography is already well established and the results are often questionable because amateurs don't see what they're doing wrong – and wouldn't know how to fix it if they did. In this way, everyone becomes accustomed to incorrect or bad typography.

When one explains, however, what constitutes good typography, people will start to get a feel for it. They will notice when something's not working or communicating effectively and will learn to recognize and appreciate the work of professionals. They will become aware that there are many areas in which professional graphic designers have a superior knowledge – but that there are also areas in which a beginner may operate with success. *Getting it Right with Type* cannot and should not replace the professional study of typography. Rather, it is intended to serve to explain the basics and ensure that the worst mistakes are avoided.

The objection could now be raised that typography is just a matter of taste. If typographic design were merely an issue of decoration, then this argument could be allowed to pass, but typography is first and foremost about the communication of information. Some errors can result in poor readability as they not only distrupt but even do damage to the content.

The correct choice of design method is a precondition for usable typo-graphy, as is the correct implementation of the method. For this there are basic rules. These rules help ensure that texts are read in the correct way, that they are easily understood and that there is no confusion. An em dash, for example, is not a hyphen. The typewriter, because of its simplifed char-acter set, drew no distinction between the two and spoiled our awareness of the difference. Now, in the age of the computer, we are able to remedy such problems. *Getting it Right with Type* will not only explain the rules, but point out the common errors and their remedies.

Anyone who studies modern typography carefully will observe violations of the rules, again and again, even in professional work. This might bring one to the conclusion that many graphic designers have a poor command of typography. It might also appear that some typographers intentionally ignore the rules. However, it is essential to point out that you first have to get the hang of the rules and understand how communication works in order to acquire the knowledge and confidence to know when you can bend or break them.

When you learn to cook, you don't start with a soufflé – it's better to try an omelette first. The same principle applies to learning typography: it is best not to start with the fancy tricks, even though the computer tempts you to do so. Circular type, shadowing, type-on-a-path, layering, positive-negative play, perspective distortions and all the other amazing opportunities that the software offers should be avoided until you have mastered the basics.

So how do you recognize whether a piece of typography is successful? By looking, observing, questioning. Is it communicating the content? Is it fit for its purpose? Does it meet the needs of the end user?

This book offers an introduction to the basics of typography: choice of typeface, typographic detailing, type applications, type with image, type and layout, paper, reproduction, print and type on screen. The main focus of *Getting it Right with Type* is how do I design this, what is the best way of designing with type, is it communicating effectively?

Those searching through *Getting it Right with Type* for tricks will search in vain, as the main aim of the book is to encourage an awareness of good typography, not to teach gimmicks.

In the days when typography was done only by typesetters (with several years of study before practising) a specialist terminology developed – a kind of secret language of the guild – using words such as 'orphans' and 'widows', which excluded the layman. Today specialist language is still used and has even been expanded due to the use of computers. Explanation of the technical terminology used within this book is found at the beginning of each chapter with an additional terminology section on page 166.

Throughout the book there are typographic examples based on actual published materials which are predominantly warnings rather than positive examples. These are used to demonstrate where problems have occurred in order to assist you in knowing what not to do.

Typography is a fascinating topic that has engrossed the lives of many. You may wish to study the topic further and for this reason there is a list on page 171 of publications and other resources to complement or continue your studies.

# Typography

## Letterforms and typefaces

Covering:
Typographic terminology
Typefaces
Type families
Type classification
Differentiating typefaces
Readability and legibility
Mixing typefaces
Numbers and figures

# What is typography?

Typography is the mechanical arrangement and organization of written words in such a way as to facilitate communication of the content.

The term 'type' traditionally refers to metal type, the physical object, where letterforms are handset and printed. However, the scope of typography has expanded on account of the development of digital technology, the use of personal computers and the growth of the Internet.

Typography is all around us, on signage, in timetables, in books, on packaging, within advertising... indeed, there are endless variations of typographic manifestations. To evaluate these, we use one criterion: the purpose determines the design.

Typography can be divided into two areas:
1. The concept / idea, the arrangement, the design as a whole. Consideration should be given to the choice of output (printed or screen-based) format, typeface(s), colour, stock (if appropriate) and composition. The term macrotypography has become widely accepted for this activity.
2. The space between the letters, between the words and lines – the details of typesetting. For this, we use the term microtypography.

Letterpress, metal typesetting.

The following examples demonstrate that well-considered typography that serves its purpose is a prerequisite for successful communication.

Showing quickly how to get from A to B.

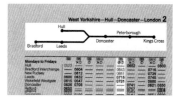

Enticement to read.

To attract by amusement.

To capture nuances.

To be recognizable at a glance (Norwegian license plate).

To put new typographic ways to the test.

To break the bonds of typography.

Proclaiming the power of belief.

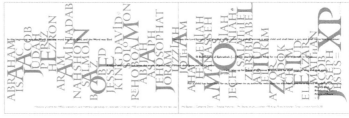

A Dutch tax form (if only ours looked so good!).

To represent, to remind, and to perform function.

To attract by scale.

To capture atmosphere.

# Letterforms:
# technical terminology

The following section gives an overview of the technical terminology used in typography. It is important to familiarize yourself with these terms as some will be referred to within this book.

Baseline

**Baseline**
An imaginary line on which the capital and lowercase letters sit.

Median

**Median**
The imaginary line which defines the x-height.

Cap Height

**Cap height**
The height of capital letterforms.

The x-height

**x-height**
The height of the lowercase x.

Uppercase

**Uppercase character**
Capital letterforms.

Lowercase

**Lowercase character**
Small letterforms, not capitals.

bdfhklt

**Ascender characters**
Lowercase letterforms with ascenders (strokes rising above the main body of the letters).

gjpqy

**Descender characters**
Lowercase letterforms with descenders (strokes extending below the main body of the letters).

abcABC

**Stroke**
A line that defines the basic letterform.

| A | E | b | S | T |
|---|---|---|---|---|
| apex | arm | ascender | barb | stem |
| crossbar | beak | bowl | spine | bracket |
| serif | | | | |

| f | V | y | i | g |
|---|---|---|---|---|
| finial | crotch | descender | dot | ear |
| cross stroke | vertex | | | link |
| | | | | loop |

| 5 | K | fi | a | h |
|---|---|---|---|---|
| flag | leg | ligature | sans serif | shoulder |
| terminal | | | | |

q

spur

O*e*

stress

## Typographic measurement

Letterforms were originally cast onto pieces of lead, and the body of the type (the surface on which the letterform stood) was measured to determine the size. The unit used for the measurement of letterforms is the 'point'.

Point size
(72pt = 1inch)

A point is equivalent to $1/72$ of an inch (0.35mm); therefore 1 inch is the equivalent of 72 points.

The spacing between the lines of letters is referred to as leading (pronounced 'ledding'), because it was originally made by inserting strips of lead; it is also measured in points (see also p.78).

Note that points and leading are written as follows when specifying type:

10/12 Helvetica

meaning 10pt (point) Helvetica with 2pt leading.

*A*

swash

Q

tail

G

throat

P

counter

# Typefaces

The term typeface is used to describe a complete alphabet including letters, numerals, punctuation marks, accents, special reference marks etc. It is important that the whole typeface is used when designing to ensure consistency.

## Uppercase and lowercase

The term uppercase originates from traditional metal typesetting. Two wooden cases were used to store the metal type, the top one for capital letters and the bottom one for small letters, hence the term uppercase and lowercase.

A B C D E F G H I J K L M N O P
Q R S T U V W X Y Z
Å Á À Â Ä Ã Ç É È Ê Ë Í Ì Î Ï Ñ
Ó Ò Ô Ö Ø Õ Ú Ù Û Ü Ÿ
a b c d e f g h i j k l m n o p q r s t u
v w x y z
å á à â ä ã ç é è ê ë í ì î ï ñ ó ò ô ö ø
õ ú ù û ü ÿ

## Small caps

True small capitals have the form of uppercase but the size (same x-height) and function of lowercase letters. They are often used alongside figures or lowercase letterforms, giving the page uniformity.

Words set in capitals or in small capitals, as they come directly out of the computer, usually appear too tightly packed against each other. This results in disturbing dark patches in the text. They should have tiny spaces inserted between them to make them more agreeable to the eye, the practice know as letterspacing.

A B C D E F G H I J K L M N O P Q R S
T U V W X Y Z
Å Á À Â Ä Ã Ç É È Ê Ë Í Ì Î Ï Ñ Ó Ò Ô
Ö Ø Õ Ú Ù Û Ü Ÿ

## Figures

Lining figures have the same height as uppercase letterforms.

## FIGURE 1 2 3 4 5 6 7 8 9 0

Non-lining figures have ascenders and descenders and are set to the same x-height as the lowercase letterforms.

## Figure 1 2 3 4 5 6 7 8 9 0

## Punctuation

Typefaces have punctuation as standard; however, additional characters can change depending upon typeface choice.

. : , ; ... ! ? / ' " [ ] { } ( ) ' " - – < >

## Dingbats

Dingbats (symbols and ornaments) are designed to use with typefaces.

## Type families

A type family consists of a number of typefaces which are related to one another. For example, the type family Century consists of typefaces such as Century Nova, Century Old Style and Century Schoolbook.

## Font

The term 'font' relates to a specific size and style of a given typeface.

## Type styles

Type styles are used to enable designers to place emphasis on a particular word, phrase, title etc, giving flexibility and enabling a hierarchy to be distinguished. The following examples show the most common styles available. Note that different terminology is used for some typefaces. For instance, italic can be called 'oblique', extended can be 'expanded', semi-bold can be 'demibold', condensed can be 'compact' (with very condensed styles being termed 'compressed') and bold can be 'medium'. The term 'book' can be used to describe letterforms that are slightly lighter than roman. These terms are sometimes used when a roman style is changed via computer software.

# Roman

Roman is the most widely used type style.

# *Italic*

Italic was originally based on handwriting, and, again, is widely used. (Note that an electronically sloped roman is not a true italic.)

# Condensed

These typefaces are used when space is at a premium.

# Extended

Extended is rarely used for longer texts due to legibility issues.

The following examples show further variations, this time in the quality known as 'weight', which refers to the density or the lightness of the individual letterforms.

# Thin
# Light
# **Bold**
# **Extrabold**

# Differentiating typefaces / type classification

### Humanist

Examples include Schneidler, Verona, Centaur and Kennerley.

Formally known as Venetian, and originating in the 15th century, typefaces within this classification have varying stroke thicknesses deriving from the broad-edged oblique pen used for calligraphy during this period.

abcd
ABCDR

### Old face

Examples include Bembo, Caslon, Dante, Garamond and Palatino.

These typefaces have broad pen-like strokes giving a greater contrast in stroke weight than the humanist typefaces. This classification is also known as old style (US) or Garalde.

abcd
ABCDR

### Script

Examples include Palace Script, Kuenstler and Mistral.

These were originally typefaces based on calligraphic forms.

### Transitional

Examples include Baskerville, Bulmer and Century. Typefaces classified in this group have a nearly vertical axis and high stroke contrast.

abcd
ABCDR

These pages are merely a brief overview of type classification. To gain further knowledge of classification systems investigate the Vox classification system, originated by the French typographic historian Maximilian Vox in 1954–5 and The British Standards *Classification of Typefaces* (BS 2961:1967).

## Modern
Examples include Bell, Bodoni and Walbaum.
Modern typefaces have strong thick–thin contrast, vertical stress, fine serifs. This classification is also known as Didone.

abcd
ABCDR

## Slab serif
Examples include Clarendon, Memphis and Rockwell. This category of typeface has even stroke weights and heavy serifs. This classification is also known as Egyptian.

abcd
ABCDR

## Sans serif
Examples include Gill Sans, Frutiger, Futura, Helvetica, Meta and Univers.
These typefaces have (almost) even stroke weights and are without serifs. This classification is also known as Lineale or Gothic (US).

abcd
ABCDR

A call to action!

FF SALE · DESIGNED BY TONY BOOTH 1996 · DISTRIBUTED EXCLUSIVELY BY FONTSHOP INTERNATIONAL

The solemn captivation of trust.

**A grant danse macabree des hômes ⁊ des femmes hystoriee ⁊ augmentee de beaulx ditz en latin.**

This typeface was derived from the manuscript tradition but now has associations with Germany during the Second World War. It is also suggestive of a traditional newspaper masthead.

# Using typefaces

Today's designer has a huge choice of typefaces: there are literally thousands! The difference between them can be extremely slight, perhaps just a larger x-height, a longer ascender or descender or a slightly different-shaped serif.

This section gives the designer an overview of the subtleties of using typefaces, the effects that they have on the reader and what the style of the typeface communicates. It is the designer's job to ensure that typefaces are used appropriately and effectively and that suitability of purpose is carefully considered.

## The effects of type

Type has a dual purpose: we see it and are affected by its aesthetics, as well as reading its forms. We have been influenced by type for thousands of years. Imperial orders, the solemn captivation of trust, the promise of casual relaxation, security, awe-demanding distance – type can disseminate all of these. Most people are unaware of these effects, but they are there nonetheless.

A relaxing, casual and friendly environment.

The effects arise, on the one hand, from the abstract form of the letters, whether soft, round, delicate, hard, elegant or rough. They come about also through what the typeface has been used for. For example, association with Hitler's National Socialists (Nazis) clings like a bad smell to Gothic, or blackletter, an otherwise innocent category of typeface originating in northern Europe in the early modern era.

There is also the subjective opinion: 'I don't like this typeface.' 'That one really appeals to me.' These are irrefutable and legitimate arguments. They do not, however, answer the more important questions for design: does this face suit the purpose, can it carry out the assignment?

A youthful and energetic typeface.

# Choice of typeface

Who would you choose to build your house?

The following examples show the same text with the same typographic treatment in four different typefaces that create four different effects.

Together they demonstrate that the message can be altered through the choice of typeface alone.

Patricia Brown
Thomas Brown
Architects

Specialists in private residential housing

Advice, planning, budgeting,
project management

Telephone 01752 245698
Fax 01752 245699
www.architects@yahoo.com

Patricia Brown
Thomas Brown
Architects

Specialists in private residential housing

Advice, planning, budgeting,
project management

Telephone 01752 245698
Fax 01752 245699
www.architects@yahoo.com

Patricia Brown
Thomas Brown
Architects

Specialists in private residential housing

Advice, planning, budgeting,
project management

Telephone 01752 245698
Fax 01752 245699
www.architects@yahoo.com

Patricia Brown
Thomas Brown
Architects

Specialists in private residential housing

Advice, planning, budgeting,
project management

Telephone 01752 245698
Fax 01752 245699
www.architects@yahoo.com

# The visual
# tone of
# typography

These examples show the same
text in the same typeface but
with four different typographic
treatments. The designer can
communicate to the audience not
only through choice of typeface,
but also through the layout of
the typography.

OUR FATHER who art in heaven,
Hallowed be thy name.
Thy kingdom come,
Thy will be done,
On earth as it is in heaven.
Give us this day our daily bread;
And forgive us our trespasses
As we forgive them who trespass against us;
And lead us not into temptation,
But deliver us from evil.
For thine is the kingdom, the power and the glory,
For ever and ever.
Amen

*Matthew 6:9-13*

OUR FATHER who art in heaven,
        Hallowed be thy name.
Thy kingdom come,
        Thy will be done,
            On earth as it is in heaven.
Give us this day our daily bread;
And forgive us our trespasses
As we forgive them who trespass against us;
And lead us not into temptation,
        But deliver us from evil.
For thine is the kingdom, the power and the glory,
        For ever and ever.
Amen

*Matthew 6:9-13*

OUR FATHER who art in heaven,
Hallowed be thy name.
Thy kingdom come,
Thy will be done,
On earth as it is in heaven.
Give us this day our daily bread;
And forgive us our trespasses
As we forgive them who trespass against us;
And lead us not into temptation,
But deliver us from evil.
For thine is the kingdom, the power and the glory,
For ever and ever.
Amen

*Matthew 6:9-13*

---

OUR FATHER who art in heaven, Hallowed be thy name. Thy kingdom come, Thy will be done, On earth as it is in heaven. Give us this day our daily bread; And forgive us our trespasses As we forgive them who trespass against us; And lead us not into temptation, But deliver us from evil. For thine is the kingdom, the power and the glory, For ever and ever. Amen

*Matthew 6:9-13*

# Recognizing typefaces

A g is not a g is not a g.

How many different typefaces can you recognize? It's amazing how 'type-blind' most of us are.

Typography has many faces but most people don't notice. If the message can be read why worry about the messenger?

It is worth studying the various characters to become aquainted with the variety of typefaces. A successful designer is effective in communicating 'non-verbally' with others.

g g R R
g g R R
g g R R
g g R R
g g R R
g g R R

It would be a great advantage if we could rely on typeface names; however this is not the case.

These three typefaces are all called Bodoni but appear quite different.

Bodoni
Bodoni
Bodoni

Conversely, some faces appear under different names. Optima is also called Octavo or Zapf Humanist; Univers once made an appearance as Galaxy.

# Typography
# and typeface

Which restaurant would you choose to eat in based on the presentation of their menu?

These four examples show the same menu with different typefaces and typographic treatment.

This is enough to change one's expectations, even without the influence of the menu's size, the paper it's printed on or the colour.

**Starters**
Butternut squash and sweet potato soup
Crab and tomato salad
Red onion, tomato and goat's cheese tart

**Main courses**
Pan-seared salmon with spinach and lemon butter
Rib-eye steak with tomato, mushroom and thin-cut fries
Basil gnocchi with parmesan and baby spinach

**Desserts**
Bread and butter pudding
Chocolate truffle cheesecake
Raspberry sorbet

Chef's selection of cheeses with port

*Starters*
Butternut squash and sweet potato soup
Crab and tomato salad
Red onion, tomato and goat's cheese tart

*Main courses*
Pan-seared salmon with spinach and lemon butter
Rib-eye steak with tomato, mushroom and thin-cut fries
Basil gnocchi with parmesan and baby spinach

*Desserts*
Bread and butter pudding
Chocolate truffle cheesecake
Raspberry sorbet

Chef's selection of cheeses with port

STARTERS
Butternut squash and sweet potato soup
Crab and tomato salad
Red onion, tomato and goat's cheese tart

MAIN COURSES
Pan-seared salmon with spinach and lemon butter
Rib-eye steak with tomato, mushroom and thin-cut fries
Basil gnocchi with parmesan and baby spinach

DESSERTS
Bread and butter pudding
Chocolate truffle cheesecake
Raspberry sorbet

Chef's selection of cheeses with port

---

STARTERS
Butternut squash and sweet potato soup
Crab and tomato salad
Red onion, tomato and goat's cheese tart

MAIN COURSES
Pan-seared salmon with spinach and lemon butter
Rib-eye steak with tomato, mushroom and thin-cut fries
Basil gnocchi with parmesan and baby spinach

DESSERTS
Bread and butter pudding
Chocolate truffle cheesecake
Raspberry sorbet

Chef's selection of cheeses with port

# Typefaces
# in a comparison of
# letterform combinations

The following examples illustrate basic critical letter combinations
and begin to demonstrate the difficulties in reading them.

Illuminated learning encourages richness

Illuminated learning encourages richness

Illuminated learning encourages richness

Illuminated learning encourages richness

Illuminated learning encourages richness

Illuminated learning encourages richness

Illuminated learning encourages richness

Illuminated learning encourages richness

Illuminated learning encourages richness

Illuminated learning encourages richness

Illuminated learning encourages richness

Illuminated learning encourages richness

Do not assume that letterforms of a simple design will be the most legible.
The answer is to identify the visually clearest letterform combinations.
It is important to consider the paper stock that letterforms will be printed on
(see p.135). This is when differentiation problems become most noticeable
(especially with faxed or photocopied text).

Reduced to 12 point, the readability issues become more apparent. The
critical letter combinations in the various typefaces are compared overleaf.

Avant Garde

Illuminated learning encourages richness

Futura

Illuminated learning encourages richness

Helvetica

Illuminated learning encourages richness

Frutiger

Illuminated learning encourages richness

Gill

Illuminated learning encourages richness

Officina Sans

Illuminated learning encourages richness

Bodoni

Illuminated learning encourages richness

Times

Illuminated learning encourages richness

Garamond

Illuminated learning encourages richness

Palatino

Illuminated learning encourages richness

Excelsior

Illuminated learning encourages richness

Rockwell

**Illuminated learning encourages richness**

| | Risk of error | | Run-together risk | |
|---|---|---|---|---|
| Avant Garde | ll | very great | rn | great |
| Futura | ll | great | rn | very great |
| Helvetica | ll | very great | rn | great |
| Frutiger | ll | great | rn | great |
| Gill | ll | very great | rn | great |
| Officina Sans | Il | minor | rn | very great |
| Bodoni | Il | great | rn | great |
| Times | Il | minor | rn | very great |
| Garamond | Il | minor | rn | great |
| Palatino | Il | great | rn | great |
| Excelsior | Il | minor | rn | very great |
| Rockwell | Il | great | rn | minor |

Typefaces in a comparison of letterform combinations

| Proportion | | Similarity | |
|---|---|---|---|
| hn | ambiguous | adg | very great |
| hn | clear | adg | great |
| hn | ambiguous | adg | minor |
| hn | clear | adg | insignificant |
| hn | clear | adg | insignificant |
| hn | clear | adg | minor |
| hn | very clear | adg | insignificant |
| hn | clear | adg | insignificant |
| hn | very clear | adg | insignificant |
| hn | clear | adg | insignificant |
| hn | clear | adg | minor |
| hn | ambiguous | adg | insignificant |

# Designing
# readable text

As a designer, if you are only asked to make the text readable on the page, the following questions should be asked:

Who is to read it?
A professional reader or a beginner? Someone who *wants* to read or someone who *has* to read?

How will it be read?
Quickly, in passing, or focused on the message?

Which typographic means are appropriate?
Perky and lively or down-to-earth; active or reserved and unobtrusive?

How should these means be applied?
As the content of the text is of paramount importance, the viewer must be able to read it easily.

The following five examples look at the communication of the text, without creative ambition, and show how the correct or incorrect use of type can ease or hinder reading.

This is dummy text. It is not meant to be read for content, but rather to create an even texture in order to evaluate typefaces more easily. One may, at a glance, quickly judge the 'colour', or grey value, of a typeface using such a text. Then one may check how easily readable a text is and how it affects the reader. One may measure how wide or narrow it sets and, upon closer examination, recognize individual letters and their quirks or special features. As one compares typefaces more and more often, one is eventually able to identify and name them. Of course, this requires attention to detail and practice.

A typeface with readability issues is also set badly – too tight, too dense.

This is dummy text. It is not meant to be read for content, but rather to create an even texture in order to evaluate typefaces more easily. One may, at a glance, quickly judge the 'colour', or grey value, of a typeface using such a text. Then one may check how easily readable a text is and how it affects the reader. One may measure how wide or narrow it sets and, upon closer examination, recognize individual letters and their quirks or special features. As one compares typefaces more and more often, one is eventually able to identify and name them. Of course, this requires attention to detail and practice.

Here the lines are somewhat clearer but this not-so-reader-friendly typeface is set far too tightly.

This is dummy text. It is not meant to be read for content, but rather to create an even texture in order to evaluate typefaces more easily. One may, at a glance, quickly judge the 'colour', or grey value, of a typeface using such a text. Then one may check how easily readable a text is and how it affects the reader. One may measure how wide or narrow it sets and, upon closer examination, recognize individual letters and their quirks or special features. As one compares typefaces more and more often, one is eventually able to identify and name them. Of course, this requires attention to detail and practice.

This example is better than the previous one but not yet ideal. The larger typesize needs more room.

This is dummy text. It is not meant to be read for content, but rather to create an even texture in order to evaluate typefaces more easily. One may, at a glance, quickly judge the 'colour', or grey value, of a typeface using such a text. Then one may check how easily readable a text is and how it affects the reader. One may measure how wide or narrow it sets and, upon closer examination, recognize individual letters and their quirks or special features. As one compares typefaces more and more often, one is eventually able to identify and name them. Of course, this requires attention to detail and practice.

In spite of its small size, this text is easily readable. This is a result not only of a good typeface, but also how it is set.

This is dummy text. It is not meant to be read for content, but rather to create an even texture in order to evaluate typefaces more easily. One may, at a glance, quickly judge the 'colour', or grey value, of a typeface using such a text. Then one may check how easily readable a text is and how it affects the reader. One may measure how wide or narrow it sets and, upon closer examination, recognize individual letters and their quirks or special features. As one compares typefaces more and more often, one is eventually able to identify and name them. Of course, this requires attention to detail and practice.

A wrong, namely too narrow, typeface, set badly: lines too long, not enough line space.

The following examples show that the use of tried and true typefaces with good reputations don't necessarily guarantee good readability. It's not difficult to make a good typeface read badly.

Helvetica had been a popular type-face for decades. Although it is not necessarily successful when used in long texts, it can nevertheless be employed effectively.

This is dummy text. It is not meant to be read for content, but rather to create an even texture in order to evaluate typefaces more easily. One may, at a glance, quickly judge the 'colour', or grey value, of a typeface using such a text. Then one may check how easily readable a text is and how it affects the reader. One may measure how wide or narrow it sets and, upon closer examination, recognize individual letters and their quirks or special features. As one compares typefaces more and more often, one is eventually able to identify and name them. Of course, this requires attention to detail and practice.

This example demonstrates that Helvetica can have poor legibility through bad setting, which results in a dense and blotchy appearance where the eyes get caught on the words. The reason is that the letters are too close together, the words are too far apart and the lines are too tight.

This is dummy text. It is not meant to be read for content, but rather to create an even texture in order to evaluate type-faces more easily. One may, at a glance, quickly judge the 'colour', or grey value of a typeface using such a text. Then one may check how easily readable a text is and how it affects the reader. One may measure how wide or narrow it sets and, upon closer examination, recognize individual letters and their quirks or special features. As one compares typefaces more and more often, one is eventually able to identify and name them. Of course, this requires attention to detail and practice.

Once again Helvetica. This is easier to read because of good setting. The visual effect is restful, and the eye of the reader is not distracted. The spacing between the letters, words and lines is co-ordinated.

Designing readable text

This is dummy text. It is not meant to be read for content, but rather to create an even texture in order to evaluate typefaces more easily. One may, at a glance, quickly judge the 'colour', or grey value, of a typeface using such a text. Then one may check how easily readable a text is and how it affects the reader. One may measure how wide or narrow it sets and, upon closer examination, recognize individual letters and their quirks or special features. As one compares typefaces more and more often, one is eventually able to identify and name them. Of course, this requires attention to detail and practice.

Although Garamond has a reputation for being indestructible, it is possible to use it badly. The effect here is too open: the eye swims over the surface instead of being able to follow the lines. The relationship between the letter-, word-, and line spacing is unco-ordinated.

This is dummy text. It is not meant to be read for content, but rather to create an even texture in order to evaluate typefaces more easily. One may, at a glance, quickly judge the 'colour', or grey value, of a typeface using such a text. Then one may check how easily readable a text is and how it affects the reader. One may measure how wide or narrow it sets and, upon closer examination, recognize individual letters and their quirks or special features. As one compares typefaces more and more often, one is eventually able to identify and name them. Of course, this requires attention to detail and practice.

Once again Garamond, this time set the way it should be. The words can be grasped as units; the lines lead the eye.

Garamond, an established benchmark of legibility for centuries, can still be spoiled by bad typography.

# Typefaces
# in a comparison
# of readability

The following examples demonstrate readability issues within certain typefaces and aim to encourage critical thinking when using the huge variety of typefaces available today.

**Avant Garde**
Not appropriate for longer texts. It is suitable for a few words at a time, particularly in capitals.

This is dummy text. It is not meant to be read for content, but rather to create an even texture in order to evaluate typefaces more easily. One may, at a glance, quickly judge the 'colour', or grey value, of a typeface using such a text. Then one may check how easily readable a text is and how it affects the reader. One may measure how wide or narrow it sets and, upon closer examination, recognize individual letters and their quirks or special features. As one compares typefaces more and more often, one is eventually able to identify and name them. Of course, this requires attention to detail and practice.

**Futura**
Well-proportioned, but problematic for the formation of word images as the round letterforms do not unite well into word images. The t is a 'stopper' in the middle of a word.

This is dummy text. It is not meant to be read for content, but rather to create an even texture in order to evaluate typefaces more easily. One may, at a glance, quickly judge the 'colour', or grey value, of a typeface using such a text. Then one may check how easily readable a text is and how it affects the reader. One may measure how wide or narrow it sets and, upon closer examination, recognize individual letters and their quirks or special features. As one compares typefaces more and more often, one is eventually able to identify and name them. Of course, this requires attention to detail and practice. This is

**Helvetica**
World-famous but not absolutely readable; suitable for shorter texts. In longer texts, the picket-fence effect slows the flow of reading.

This is dummy text. It is not meant to be read for content, but rather to create an even texture in order to evaluate typefaces more easily. One may, at a glance, quickly judge the 'colour', or grey value, of a typeface using such a text. Then one may check how easily readable a text is and how it affects the reader. One may measure how wide or narrow it sets and, upon closer examination, recognize individual letters and their quirks or special features. As one compares typefaces more and more often, one is eventually able to identify and name them. Of course, this requires attention to detail and practice. This is dummy text. It is not meant to be read for content.

This is dummy text. It is not meant to be read for content, but rather to create an even texture in order to evaluate typefaces more easily. One may, at a glance, quickly judge the 'colour', or grey value, of a typeface using such a text. Then one may check how easily readable a text is and how it affects the reader. One may measure how wide or narrow it sets and, upon closer examination, recognize individual letters and their quirks or special features. As one compares typefaces more and more often, one is eventually able to identify and name them. Of course, this requires attention to detail and practice. This is dummy text.

Gill
One of the most readable sans serifs with unambiguous letterforms and optimal guidance along the lines.

This is dummy text. It is not meant to be read for content, but rather to create an even texture in order to evaluate type-faces more easily. One may, at a glance, quickly judge the 'colour', or grey value, of a typeface using such a text. Then one may check how easily readable a text is and how it affects the reader. One may measure how wide or narrow it sets and, upon closer examination, recognize individual letters and their quirks or special features. As one compares typefaces more and more often, one is eventually able to identify and name them. Of course, this requires attention to detail and practice.

Frutiger
A good, readable face, polished and mature.

This is dummy text. It is not meant to be read for content, but rather to create an even texture in order to evaluate typefaces more easily. One may, at a glance, quickly judge the 'colour', or grey value, of a typeface using such a text. Then one may check how easily readable a text is and how it affects the reader. One may measure how wide or narrow it sets and, upon closer examination, recognize individual letters and their quirks or special features. As one compares typefaces more and more often, one is eventually able to identify and name them. Of course, this requires attention to detail and practice. This is dummy text.

Officina Sans
A sans serif with serifs, durable and fairly readable.

**Bodoni**

An awkward case. It is a celebrated and beautiful roman face with unambiguous letterforms, but it doesn't guide the eye along the line. The vertical dominates, hence it requires healthy line spacing.

This is dummy text. It is not meant to be read for content, but rather to create an even texture in order to evaluate typefaces more easily. One may, at a glance, quickly judge the 'colour', or grey value, of a typeface using such a text. Then one may check how easily readable a text is and how it affects the reader. One may measure how wide or narrow it sets and, upon closer examination, recognize individual letters and their quirks or special features. As one compares typefaces more and more often, one is eventually able to identify and name them. Of course, this requires attention to detail and practice. This is dummy text. It is not meant to be read for content.

**Times**

One of the most popular, most used and functional typefaces of the 20th century.

This is dummy text. It is not meant to be read for content, but rather to create an even texture in order to evaluate typefaces more easily. One may, at a glance, quickly judge the 'colour', or grey value, of a typeface using such a text. Then one may check how easily readable a text is and how it affects the reader. One may measure how wide or narrow it sets and, upon closer examination, recognize individual letters and their quirks or special features. As one compares typefaces more and more often, one is eventually able to identify and name them. Of course, this requires attention to detail and practice. This is dummy text. It is not meant to be read for content, but rather to create an even texture.

**Garamond**

One of the most used and reliable literary faces.

This is dummy text. It is not meant to be read for content, but rather to create an even texture in order to evaluate typefaces more easily. One may, at a glance, quickly judge the 'colour', or grey value, of a typeface using such a text. Then one may check how easily readable a text is and how it affects the reader. One may measure how wide or narrow it sets and, upon closer examination, recognize individual letters and their quirks or special features. As one compares typefaces more and more often, one is eventually able to identify and name them. Of course, this requires attention to detail and practice. This is dummy text. It is not meant to be read for content.

This is dummy text. It is not meant to be read for content, but rather to create an even texture in order to evaluate typefaces more easily. One may, at a glance, quickly judge the 'colour', or grey value, of a typeface using such a text. Then one may check how easily readable a text is and how it affects the reader. One may measure how wide or narrow it sets and, upon closer examination, recognize individual letters and their quirks or special features.  As one compares typefaces more and more often, one is eventually able to identify and name them. Of course, this requires attention to detail and practice. This is dummy text. It is not meant to be read for content.

Palatino
A good, readable typeface from the 1950s. Its origins in writing with the broad pen are distinctive, hence the calligraphic elegance.

This is dummy text. It is not meant to be read for content, but rather to create an even texture in order to evaluate type-faces more easily. One may, at a glance, quickly judge the 'colour', or grey value, of a typeface using such a text. Then one may check how easily readable a text is and how it affects the reader. One may measure how wide or narrow it sets and, upon closer examination, recognize individual letters and their quirks or special features. As one compares typefaces more and more often, one is eventually able to identify and name them. Of course, this requires attention to detail.

Excelsior
A virtually indestructible newspaper typeface, created for use in situations where printing quality cannot be guaranteed.

This is dummy text. It is not meant to be read for content, but rather to create an even texture in order to evaluate typefaces more easily. One may, at a glance, quickly judge the 'colour', or grey value, of a typeface using such a text. Then one may check how easily readable a text is and how it affects the reader. One may measure how wide or narrow it sets and, upon closer examination, recognize individual letters and their quirks or special features. As one compares typefaces more and more often, one is eventually able to identify and name them. Of course, this requires attention to detail and practice. This is dummy text. It is not meant to be read for content.

Rockwell Light
A typeface with strong serifs, yielding good line-flow, but with a certain harshness.

# Reading
# narrow
# typefaces

Condensed typefaces are often chosen when there is not much space so that the letters can still be reasonably large. Whether this aids readability is open to question. Equally, narrow typefaces and long lines (wide columns) do not work well together.

## sometimes

## sometimes

This picket fence is the mid-zone of a word set in Akzidenz Grotesk Condensed.

The same mid-zone, set in normal Akzidenz Grotesk.

This is dummy text. It is not meant to be read for content, but rather to create an even texture in order to evaluate typefaces more easily. One may, at a glance, quickly judge the 'colour', or grey value, of a typeface using such a text. Then one may check how easily readable a text is and how it affects the reader. One may measure how wide or narrow it sets and, upon closer examination, recognize individual letters and their quirks or special features. As one compares typefaces more and more often, one is eventually able to identify and name them. Of course, this requires attention to detail and practice.

With some tight-fitting faces such as this Akzidenz Grotesk Condensed, it is not always clear at a glance which letters we are seeing so word forms need to be more carefully analysed. This destroys legibility in long texts as well as the recognition of single words.

This is dummy text. It is not meant to be read for content, but rather to create an even texture in order to evaluate typefaces more easily. One may, at a glance, quickly judge the 'colour', or grey value, of a typeface using such a text. Then one may check how easily readable a text is and how it affects the reader. One may measure how wide or narrow it sets and, upon closer examination, recognize individual letters and their quirks or special features. As one compares typefaces more and more often, one is eventually able to identify and name them. Of course, this requires attention to detail and practice.

Akzidenz Grotesk again. In typefaces with normal proportions, all elements of the letters give clues to their identities. This helps legibility.

In practice, most condensed faces are set justified. A rule of thumb, however, applies here: narrow setting = flush left.

This is dummy text. It is not meant to be read for content, but rather to create an even texture in order to evaluate typefaces more easily. One may, at a glance, quickly judge the 'colour', or grey value, of a typeface using such a text. Then one may check how easily readable a text is and how it affects the reader. One may measure how wide or narrow it sets and, upon closer examination, recognize individual letters and their quirks or special features. As one compares typefaces more and more often, one is eventually able to identify and name them. Of course, this requires attention to detail and practice.

This typeface, Akzidenz Grotesk Condensed, is set as large as possible to fill the area that has been given, hence it is set as tightly as possible. This does not serve legibility.

This is dummy text. It is not meant to be read for content, but rather to create an even texture in order to evaluate typefaces more easily. One may, at a glance, quickly judge the 'colour', or grey value, of a typeface using such a text. Then one may check how easily readable a text is and how it affects the reader. One may measure how wide or narrow it sets and, upon closer examination, recognize individual letters and their quirks or special features. As one compares typefaces more and more often, one is eventually able to identify and name them. Of course, this requires attention to detail and practice.

The same text in Frutiger Condensed. It doesn't run as tight as Akzidenz Grotesk Condensed and doesn't need to be set as large to fit the same area. Legibility is improved.

This is dummy text. It is not meant to be read for content, but rather to create an even texture in order to evaluate typefaces more easily. One may, at a glance, quickly judge the 'colour', or grey value, of a typeface using such a text. Then one may check how easily readable a text is and how it affects the reader. One may measure how wide or narrow it sets and, upon closer examination, recognize individual letters and their quirks or special features. As one compares typefaces more and more often, one is eventually able to identify and name them. Of course, this requires attention to detail and practice.

Once again the same text in the same area, this time set in Thesis Sans. This typeface is more expanded than Akzidenz Grotesk Condensed and Frutiger Condensed. To ensure the same text fits in the same area the typesize must be much smaller and the line spacing greater. Legibility is again improved.

This is dummy text. It is not meant to be read for content, but rather to create an even texture in order to evaluate typefaces more easily. One may, at a glance, quickly judge the 'colour', or grey value, of a typeface using such a text. Then one may check how easily readable a text is and how it affects the reader. One may measure how wide or narrow it sets and, upon closer examination, recognize individual letters and their quirks or special features. As one compares typefaces more and more often, one is eventually able to identify and name them. Of course, this requires attention to detail and practice.

For comparison, the same text set in Weidemann, an especially narrow-running face, which nevertheless remains remarkably legible.

# Mixing
# typefaces

There are no binding recipes for type combinations.
It is a matter of typographic sensitivity and experience.
Expert typographers, as well as careless amateurs,
permit themselves combinations that would horrify
colleagues with more traditional sympathies.

One can, however, gain some certainty by keeping an
eye on the characteristic shapes of letterforms.

The examples on page 45 are meant to sensitize, not to
act as rules for 'right' or 'wrong'. Hence the typeface
names are not given.

**D**er Taucher Cousteau, der
St-Exupéry des Meeres
und seiner Bewohner, ist
selbst ein Geschöpf des
Meeres, ein glitzerndes,
gleitendes, von Salzwasser ausgelaugtes
Meerwesen, ein geschmeidiger Octopus.
Die klassische Prosa dieses Sportsman-
nes lockte Scharen, mit Flossen und
Tauchermasken angetan, zu sich in die
Meerestiefen, in ein ästhetisches und ath-
letisches Abenteuer. Zunächst in ein auf-
rüttelndes Erlebnis, wenigstens für die mit
reicher Phantasie Begabten. Durch die
Vergrößerungsgläser der Taucherbrillen
sehen Elritzen wie Schwärme menschen-
fressender Raubtiere aus; umwogt von

This is a totally taboo mixture: an italic Renaissance
roman with a modern initial. It breaks all the rules.

A typographic virtuoso such as Alexey Brodovitch can
get away with it. (The example is shown at approxi-
mately 60 percent of original size.) The reason these
two typefaces don't clash in this case is the difference
in size.

The larger the contrast of size and weight, the less
important questions of style become.

This typeface wants nothing to do with its raised initial; a cold unfamiliarity prevails.

Raised initial is the term used to describe the following typographic arrangement in which the initial is larger, the text smaller. The two typefaces must nevertheless get along with each other.

Serif text type with a sans serif drop cap – compatible neverthe-less. The reason is a common stylistic derivation.

Raised initial is the term used to describe the following typographic arrangement in which the initial is larger, the text smaller. The two typefaces must nevertheless get along with each other.

Here there is a reserved coolness. The two want nothing to do with each other.

Raised initial is the term used to describe the following typographic arrangement in which the initial is larger, the text smaller. The two typefaces must nevertheless get along with each other.

An unclear relationship. Similar and yet different, both are harmed.

Raised initial is the term used to describe the following typographic arrangement in which the initial is larger, the text smaller. The two typefaces must nevertheless get along with each other.

Strictly speaking, this shouldn't work, because the combination is so foreign. But the extreme contrast of weights reduces the alienating effect.

Raised initial is the term used to describe the following typographic arrangement in which the initial is larger, the text smaller. The two typefaces must nevertheless get along with each other.

On these pages six examples of compatible and less than compatible combinations of typeface are put to the test.

## Heading

This is dummy text. It is not meant to be read for content, but rather to create an even texture in order to evaluate typefaces more easily. One may, at a glance, quickly judge the 'colour', or grey value, of a typeface using such a text. Then one may check how easily readable a text is and how it affects the reader. One may measure how wide or narrow it sets.

Two 'upright' faces. The heading is in Helvetica, the text in Walbaum, and they harmonize well.

## Heading

This is dummy text. It is not meant to be read for content, but rather to create an even texture in order to evaluate typefaces more easily. One may, at a glance, quickly judge the 'colour', or grey value, of a typeface using such a text. Then one may check how easily readable a text is and how it affects the reader. One may measure how wide or narrow it sets and, upon closer examination, recognize individual letters and their quirks or special features.

The two 'moving' faces, Gill Sans for the heading and Garamond for the text, work well together.

## Heading

This is dummy text. It is not meant to be read for content, but rather to create an even texture in order to evaluate typefaces more easily. One may, at a glance, quickly judge the 'colour', or grey value, of a typeface using such a text. Then one may check how easily readable a text is and how it affects the reader. One may measure how wide or narrow it sets and, upon closer examination, recognize individual letters and their quirks or special features.

Cross-check: Gill (in the heading) leans to the right but is stopped by Bodoni (in the text). The result is disharmony.

### Heading

This is dummy text. It is not meant to be read for content, but rather to create an even texture in order to evaluate typefaces more easily. One may, at a glance, quickly judge the 'colour', or grey value, of a typeface using such a text. Then one may check how easily readable a text is and how it affects the reader. One may measure how wide or narrow it sets and, upon closer examination, recognize individual letters and their quirks or special features.

Helvetica and Garamond are alien to each other. They have no common features, but the contrast is also not clear.

### Heading

This is dummy text. It is not meant to be read for content, but rather to create an even texture in order to evaluate typefaces more easily. One may, at a glance, quickly judge the 'colour', or grey value, of a typeface using such a text. Then one may check how easily readable a text is and how it affects the reader. One may measure how wide or narrow it sets and, upon closer examination, recognize individual letters and their quirks or special features.

Futura shows enough of its own will to contrast well with Bodoni.

### Heading

This is dummy text. It is not meant to be read for content, but rather to create an even texture in order to evaluate typefaces more easily. One may, at a glance, quickly judge the 'colour', or grey value, of a typeface using such a text. Then one may check how easily readable a text is and how it affects the reader. One may measure how wide or narrow it sets and, upon closer examination, recognize individual letters and their quirks or special features.

Futura forms an adequate contrast to Garamond as well. The encounter is, however, not so convincing.

# Condensing type

Typesetting technology permits anyone to stretch or squeeze letterforms to their heart's content. This is always, however, an attack on the substance of a typeface. Don't distort the type! It will destroy the letters.

Helvetica Condensed – made by the designer to fit in with the Helvetica family concept. Carefully balanced in proportion and stroke weight.

# Distortion

Helvetica, artificially condensed by the user. Vertical strokes are thus thinner, horizontal strokes remain as they were and have the effect of being too bold.

# Distortion

The more type is condensed, the more its forms and proportions, which were achieved with much trouble and care, are distorted.

# Distortion

As Adrian Frutiger demonstrated, it's like elongating the Mona Lisa. Although not as extreme, even minimal distortions damage the typeface.

# Distortion

This is dummy text. It is not meant to be read for content, but rather to create an even texture in order to evaluate typefaces more easily. One may, at a glance, quickly judge the 'colour', or grey value, of a typeface using such a text. Then one may check how easily readable a text is and how it affects the reader. One may measure how wide or narrow it sets and, upon closer examination, recognize individual letters and their quirks or special features.

Helvetica Condensed again, as drawn by the designer.

This is dummy text. It is not meant to be read for content, but rather to create an even texture in order to evaluate typefaces more easily. One may, at a glance, quickly judge the 'colour', or grey value, of a typeface using such a text. Then one may check how easily readable a text is and how it affects the reader. One may measure how wide or narrow it sets and, upon closer examination, recognize individual letters and their quirks or special features.

Helvetica, this time electronically condensed. While at larger sizes one can see what havoc is wreaked, at smaller sizes one can only sense it.

This is dummy text. It is not meant to be read for content, but rather to create an even texture in order to evaluate typefaces more easily. One may, at a glance, quickly judge the 'colour', or grey value, of a typeface using such a text. Then one may check how easily readable a text is and how it affects the reader. One may measure how wide or narrow it sets and, upon closer examination, recognize individual letters and their quirks or special features.

This example shows the space-saving version of Concorde Nova, created by G. G. Lange in 1975.

This is dummy text. It is not meant to be read for content, but rather to create an even texture in order to evaluate typefaces more easily. One may, at a glance, quickly judge the 'colour', or grey value, of a typeface using such a text. Then one may check how easily readable a text is and how it affects the reader. One may measure how wide or narrow it sets and, upon closer examination, recognize individual letters and their quirks or special features.

Compare it to the electronically condensed normal Concorde.

'You were driving too fast.
'What do you mean? it says
80 there.'
'No it doesn't. It says 60.'

In the past you could have got
caught for speeding on the
European continent due to a Bold
Condensed sans serif. However,
the authorities have (for the
most part) learned their lesson,
as on newer street signs the 6
is unmistakeable.

**60 80**

60 80

# Designing
# with numbers
# and figures

Research into typeface legibility has been carried out since the 1920s. Legibility of numbers, however, has seen very little. Numbers are made up of figures, as words are made up of letters. 'Word images' stay in one's mind but 'number images' tend not to do so. The unmistakeability of figures is hence even more important than with letters.

One can recognize that in some typefaces much care has been given to integrate the figures formally with the letters, however, the form of figures has developed separately from that of letters. While our alphabet has Greek and Roman origins, our figures come from Arabic roots.

On the following pages look at some of the more distinguishing features of figures.

The subject as a whole, of course, is much more complex.

This is dummy text. It reveals a lot about the typeface in which it was set on 04.08.2005. On first sight the grey value of...

Lining figures within a line give emphasis.

This is dummy text. It reveals a lot about the typeface in which it was set on 04.08.2005. On first sight the grey value of...

Old style figures fit in well with lowercase letters.

This is dummy text[1]. It reveals a lot about the typeface in which it is set. On first sight the grey value of the type area[2] is visible. One may then establish how easily readable[3] a text is and how it affects the reader.

Reference (or superscript) figures are usually made by merely reducing the normal figures of the typeface. A few well-planned type families have their own sub- and superscript figures.

## Lining figures or modern figures

All figures have the same height, matching that of the capital letters, and align on the baseline.
These are usually used alongside uppercase letterforms or in tabular material. However, they may also be used when the designer wishes the figures to stand out from lowercase letterforms.

FIGURE 1 2 3 4 5 6 7 8 9 0

**Figure 1 2 3 4 5 6 7 8 9 0**

## Non-lining or old style figures

The figures have ascenders and descenders and are set to the x-height, corresponding to the lowercase letters. Non-lining figures are usually used, and sit comfortably alongside, lowercase letterforms or in combination with small caps. Sans serifs traditionally have not had non-lining figures. Most of the more contemporary ones do, however, which makes them more versatile.

Figure 1 2 3 4 5 6 7 8 9 0

FIGURE 1 2 3 4 5 6 7 8 9 0

# Reading numbers

'Hello, may I speak with Mrs Smith from marketing, please?'
'You probably want Colibri Associates. You're the fifth caller so far today. Instead of 427-5509, just dial 427-3509.

Recent trends in letterhead typography favour small typesizes and light grey or powder blue ink, making it difficult to differentiate between some numbers.

In the above example, the information for Colibri Associates was printed in 5-point Walbaum in which the 3 and the 5 look remarkably similar. It is therefore important to stress that when dealing with numbers aesthetics should not take precedence over function.

## Readability of figures: number grouping

Examples of grouping UK and US telephone numbers:
UK
+ 44 (0) 1392 687234
UK London
+ 44 (0) 20 8798 0946
US
+ 1 (303) 427-3509

An example of credit card number grouping for the UK and US:
2345 8786 9823 8483
(four groups of four numbers)

Examples of grouping sort codes (UK) and routing numbers (US):
Sort code:
60 59 48
(three groups of two numbers)
Routing number:
463890654
(nine consecutive numbers)

Examples of postcodes (UK) and zip codes (US):
Postcode:
EX31 7DB
Zip code:
80302
Zip code with extension:
80302-7578

Numbers up to four figures are set without spaces but can take a comma:
3000
3,000

Numbers of more than four figures can be set out with spaces, full points or commas. However, the use of spaces is the most visually elegant arrangement:
30 000
300 000
3 000 000

The two examples below demonstrate that longer numbers must be grouped to aid readability. The first is a tiny communication-hostile, set-like-a-picket-fence sans with ungrouped numbers:
Colibri Associates
385 45th St. East
Suite 819
Boulder
CO 80302
Telephone 13034273509
Fax 13034273510

The same text, this time better, with grouped numbers:
Colibri Associates
385 45th St. East
Suite 819
Boulder
CO 80302
Telephone + 1 (303) 427-3509
Fax + 1 (303) 427-3510

## Readability of figures: typeface

These examples show the importance of selecting an appropriate typeface when the readability of numbers is of importance.

Set in this minimum size, the 3 and the 5 of the otherwise beautiful Walbaum are difficult to differentiate.

Colibri Associates
385 45th St. East
Suite 819
Boulder
CO 80302
Telephone + 1 (303) 427-3509
Fax + 1 (303) 427-3510

With Bodoni, the 3 and 5 are differentiated. Nevertheless it is still challenging for the user.

Colibri Associates
385 45th St. East
Suite 819
Boulder
CO 80302
Telephone + 1 (303) 427-3509
Fax + 1 (303) 427-3510

The modern Trebuchet is set in a very small typesize with lining figures. The numbers / lines are indistinct.

Colibri Associates
385 45th St. East
Suite 819
Boulder
CO 80302
Telephone + 1 (303) 427-3509
Fax + 1 (303) 427-3510

The same text with Caslon, using non-lining figures. The numbers are more readable, the lines clearer.

Colibri Associates
385 45th St. East
Suite 819
Boulder
CO 80302
Telephone + 1 (303) 427-3509
Fax + 1 (303) 427-3510

Reader-friendly typesize of Trade Gothic Light with lining figures. The example is attractive but not very easy to read.

Colibri Associates
385 45th St. East
Suite 819
Boulder
CO 80302
Telephone + 1 (303) 427-3509
Fax + 1 (303) 427-3510

Franklin Gothic Demi.
Powerful and expressive but not easily readable.

**Colibri Associates**
**385 45th St. East**
**Suite 819**
**Boulder**
**CO 80302**
**Telephone + 1 (303) 427-3509**
**Fax + 1 (303) 427-3510**

## Readability of figures: line-spacing

In this example we show, taken from the approach used in Erik Spiekermann's *Rhyme and Reason*, a scale of typographic reader-friendliness, from annoying to agreeable. The examples demonstrate how adequate line-spacing supports legibility and should serve as self-tests for designers.

Georgia with non-lining figures set without leading.

Colibri Associates
385 45th St. East
Telephone + 1 (303) 427-3509
Fax + 1 (303) 427-3510

Georgia with leading, thus more readable:

Colibri Associates
385 45th St. East
Telephone + 1 (303) 427-3509
Fax + 1 (303) 427-3510

GroThesis with non-lining figures set without leading.

Colibri Associates
385 45th St. East
Telephone + 1 (303) 427-3509
Fax 1 (303) 427-3510

As readable as Georgia:
GroThesis non-lining figures, with leading.

Colibri Associates
385 45th St. East
Telephone + 1 (303) 427-3509
Fax + 1 (303) 427-3510

# Designing
# with words

My cultured colleagues mock every grammatical blunder that slips past the editors of popular newspapers and magazines. However, it is only my colleagues working in design who notice the typographical indiscretions in those same publications.

This section will introduce you to the basics of designing with words. It focuses on the details that should be considered when producing craftsmanlike, legible typography.

The type user should consider:

• typographic detailing that will need to be addressed

• that a suitable typeface and -size has been chosen

• the relationship of letters to each other

• the relationship of words to each other

• the relationship between word space and line space

• the relationship between typesize and line space

• the relation between column width and line space

• the choice of alignment, whether ranged left, ranged right, justified or centred

The following examples demonstrate that many type users do not have knowledge of the basic fundamentals of typography and typesetting.

## In general...............
A YEAR on from the massive flooding, residents are keeping things low key as the first anniversary approaches.

Such an obvious error – and in a headline! (See ellipsis p.60.)

To introduce you to St Lucia we include an early morning walk and, to find out more about its cuisine and rum, a chance to see typical food - and drink - being prepared, with plenty of sampling of the results! And we strongly recommend seeing more of the island, whether you hire a car and explore at your own pace or take one of the many excursions.

Misuse of hyphens. (See p.61.)

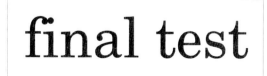

## final test

A bold error. Using a fi ligature within this headline would have made all the difference. (See p.61.)

shoes and accessories all at great prices. Lindsay will also be stocking some well-known labels for the winter season. Call in to this friendly shop and take a look for yourself.

A block of text with a widow. (See pp.65 and 91.)

Mrs Anne Kern, *2 York Street, London W6 4AU; e-mail:annekern@myemail.com*

Q I enclose a group photograph which is presumably of staff and patients at Kirkee Station Hospital, India. I think the man on the far right middle row is my grandfather, George Albert Peedle, who served with the ASC during World War I. Unfortunately I have been unable to find any service papers and presume that they were destroyed along with so many others. I have found his medal records and still have the medal.

Two typographic errors here. Small caps and lining figures would have been more sensitive (see p.52) and the line break / hyphen in email is criminal!

**AMUSEMENT PARK** is open, October through March 9-4.30pm except Sundays.Entry for under fives half-price.

Again there is misuse of a hyphen when an en rule should be used. (See p.61.) A word space is also required after the full point between Sundays and Entry. (See p.59.)

# All you can eat buffet $10.99

The descender of the 'y' overlaps the ascender of the 't'. More leading required. (See pp.63 and 78.)

- Spend as much time as you possibly can at the exhibition chatting to people you see looking at your works.
- If you put a reasonable value on your works, make sure you have them insured.

Ranged left text with problem hyphens causing poor line breaks, especially in the second bullet point. (See p.85.)

# PRIVATE

The space between the V and the A needs to be kerned.
(See p.62.)

The Show was shaping up to be a record-breaking success yesterday afternoon.

Hundreds of contestants and visitors started to pour through the gates of the aerodrome from early in the morning.

As well as crowds of spectators, there were more stalls and entrants than last year – which was itself a record-breaking event.

More than 700 people put forward their animals for the open dog show.

Justified text can cause problems with word spaces as this example clearly shows. (See p.86.)

## General Store

Poor positioning of text within a box.
(See p.94.)

in the rustic homespun and high boots of an ostler from one of the inns.

"Why . . . hello," Andrea stammered.

"Hi, Andrea. I see you went ahead with the costume I'd cooked up." He came closer, his expression unreadable in the dusky evening light. "I hoped you might."

"Oh?" Andrea's pulse quickened. "I never thanked you for the portrait. I meant to, but you were always so busy."

Again, a problem with word spacing and in particular the ellipsis.

# Words and paragraphs: technical terminology

The following pages give an overview of the technical terminology for words and paragraphs. It is important to familiarize yourself with this section, as by using and taking note of the terms and their typographic relevance it will assist you in producing typography at a more professional level.

## Punctuation

When designing with words it is vitally important that the correct punctuation is used to demonstrate pauses, inflexions and emphases and to ensure clarity when reading. There will be times when you may be working with a writer or editor who will be focusing on the correct usage. However, when a client supplies the text you do need to pay attention to the details of the words and punctuation and understand them fully.

While housestyle between publishers and organizations will vary it is important to know the basic rules on the use of punctuation. There is also a range of style manuals available if you wish to study the subject in more depth. For keyboard shortcuts to creating punctuation please refer to Appendix 1.

## full point.

The full point is otherwise known as a full stop or period. It is used to mark the end of a sentence that does not close with an exclamation or question mark. It is also used with abbreviations. It is always followed by a letter space. (See also Abbreviations, p.61.)

## comma,

The comma separates co-ordinated items and defines clauses and phrases within a sentence. For example: 'She put on her coat, which was new, and went out into the rain.' It is also used to separate items in a list.

## colon:

A colon is situated within a sentence to mark a pause indicating a step forward from introduction to main theme, from cause to effect, premiss to conclusion. It is used when the preceding part is complete both in sense and construction and the following part arises from it in sense but not in construction. For example: 'Study to acquire a habit of thinking: no habit is more important.' It is also used to indicate a list of items and after expressions such as, 'for example', 'to sum up' etc. A dash should not be added after a colon where its use is to indicate a list.

## semicolon;

The semicolon divides a sentence in cases where the sense requires a larger pause than that of a comma, but where the sentence should not be split into two as the information is closely connected. For example: 'Economy is no disgrace; for it is better to live on a little than to outlive a great deal.'

## exclamation mark!

This mark is used to indicate an exclamation of word, phrase, or sentence, expressing emotion, pain, sorrow, enthusiasm etc, and should be positioned directly after this. It should be noted that this mark is used for emphasis and should be used sparingly.

## question mark?

The question mark is used to follow every question that requires a separate answer. It is not used after an indirect question has been posed.

## (parenthesis)

Parentheses are used to enclose remarks made by the writer of the text, as well as explanations, definitions, authorities or references. Parentheses can also be used to enclose interruptions from an audience in the report of a speech, and enclosing reference letters or figures.

## [square bracket]

Square brackets are used to enclose comments, corrections, explanations, notes, questions or translations that are not in the original text, but have been added.

## pets{ cat dog

A brace is used in tabular work to connect words, lines etc. When it is used to demonstrate that one point comprises many others, the brace should point towards the single item which should be centred on it.

Braces are also used for brackets within parentheses.

## forward slash/

The forward slash is also referred to as a shilling mark or a virgule. It is now especially used to separate different elements in website addresses and dates given in numerical form. A solidus / (shift, alt, 1) is often used instead of the forward slash or virgule. A solidus is specifically used as a fraction bar.

## ellipses...

The ellipsis is a single character made up of three periods and has its own keyboard stroke (alt ;). A series of three normal periods may be used when one wishes more control over the spacing between the dots, although in that case one must ensure that the periods are not separated at line breaks. When the ellipsis stands for omitted words, it usually has a letterspace either side. When it stands for an omitted word part, the letterspaces are omitted. A period following an ellipsis must be separated from it by a letterspace.

## apostrophe'

An apostrophe is used to show an omission of a letter or letters, for example, it's for it is. It demonstrates possession or close association, for example, Mark's car. The apostrophe must not be confused with the single open quotation mark or with the signs for feet and minutes (used in longitude and latitude).

## single open quote'
## foot/minute'
## inch mark"

## hyphen-

The hyphen is used to join words to form a single expression such as rock-forming. It is also used adjectively, for example, 'a well-known painting', as opposed to 'the painting is well known'. It is also used for word breaks at the ends of lines.

## en dash –

The en dash is used to link two items together, for example as a range between dates or between places, such as: 1997–8 and the London–Manchester train. It is not to be confused with the hyphen. A hyphen is a short stroke, the en dash somewhat longer and usually thinner. In the UK a spaced en rule can be used as a parenthical dash to denote an aside.

## em dash or rule —

The em dash is used to indicate a pause in hesitant speech, for example, 'Wait—I'll come'. It can also be used in place of parentheses, especially remarks made by the writer. It tends to be used more regularly in US texts than in UK texts.

## 'single quotes'
## "double quotes"

Quotation marks, either single or double, are used to mark the beginning and end of a quoted passage, chapter of a book, title of an article and to show speech. Do not use inch or foot marks / signs in place of true quotation marks.

Quotation marks, either single or double, are used to mark the beginning and end of a quoted passage, chapter of a book, title of an article and to show speech. Do not use inch or foot marks / signs in place of true quotation marks.

## ‹guillemets›

French and Italian.

## »guillemets«

German.

Guillemets are an alternate way of indicating quotations. Note that guillemets should not be replaced by the mathematical < > signs.

## ligatures

They are designed to avoid the clash between the finial on the f and the dot of the i or with the ascender of the following f or l.

### Abbreviations
In cases where a word has been shortened a full point is used to indicate this. In this way a full point is used after personal initials, such as J. S. Smith and after abbreviations, such as Feb. for February. A full point is generally not used for contractions, such as Dr, Mrs, Mr, St, but this is often a matter of style, so check with the client. Generally acronyms in capitals do not take full points, for example USA, UK, BBC, UNICEF.

## Kerning

Some characters, when positioned next to one another, do not have the same character spacing compared to the adjacent letter-forms, such as Yo in York or AV in AVERAGE. This is due to the angled slopes of the letterforms.

Kerning is used to reduce the space between these characters to enable the space between them to remain visually consistent, improving letterfit.

AVERAGE

Without kerning.

AVERAGE

With kerning.

York

Without kerning.

York

With kerning.

AVERAGE

Without kerning.

AVERAGE

With kerning.

York

Without kerning.

York

With kerning.

## Blocks of text:
## technical terminology

The examples on this page and overleaf explain the technical terminology used when dealing with blocks of text.

This is dummy text. It is not meant to be read for content, but rather to create an even texture in order to evaluate typefaces more easily. One may, at a glance, quickly judge the 'colour', or grey value, of a typeface using such a text. Then one may check how easily readable a text is and how it affects the reader. One may measure how wide or narrow it sets and, upon closer examination, recognize individual letters and their quirks or special features. As one compares type-faces more and more often, one is eventually able to identify and name them. ¶

letterspacing

wordspacing

Of course, this requires attention to detail and practice. This is dummy text. It is not meant to be read for content, but rather to create an even texture in order to evaluate typefaces more easily. One may, at a glance, quickly judge the 'colour', or grey value, of a typeface using such a text. Then one may check how easily readable a text is and how it affects the reader. One may measure how wide or narrow it sets and, upon closer exam-ination, recognize individual letters and their quirks or special features. As one compares typefaces more and more often, one is eventually able to identify and name them. Of course, this requires attention to detail and practice.This is dummy text. It is not meant to be read for content, but rather to create an even texture in order to evaluate typefaces more easily. ¶

leading

river

pilcrow

One may, at a glance, quickly judge the 'colour', or grey value, of a typeface using such a text. Then one may check how easily readable a text is and how it affects the reader. One may measure how wide or narrow it sets. ¶

line length

This is dummy text. It is not meant to be read for content, but rather to create an even texture in order to evaluate typefaces more easily. One may, at a glance, quickly judge the 'colour', or grey value, of a typeface using such a text. Then one may check how easily readable a text is and how it affects the reader. One may measure how wide or narrow it sets and, upon closer examination, recognize individual letters and their quirks or special features. As one compares typefaces more and more often, one is eventually able to identify and name them.

Of course, this requires attention to detail and practice. This is dummy text. It is not meant to be read for content, but rather to create an even texture in order to evaluate typefaces more easily. One may, at a glance, quickly judge the 'colour', or grey value, of a typeface using such a text. Then

one may check how easily readable a text is and how it affects the reader. One may measure how wide or narrow it sets and, upon closer examination, recognize individual letters and their quirks or special features. As one compares typefaces more and more often, one is eventually able to identify and name them. Of course, this requires attention to detail and practice.

This is dummy text. It is not meant to be read for content, but rather to create an even texture in order to evaluate typefaces more easily. One may, at a glance, quickly judge the 'colour', or grey value, of a typeface using such a text. Then one may check how easily readable a text is and how it affects the reader. One may measure how wide or narrow it sets and, upon closer examination, recognize individual letters and their quirks or special features.

paragraph space

paragraph space

This is dummy text. It is not meant to be read for content, but rather to create an even texture in order to evaluate typefaces more easily. One may, at a glance, quickly judge the 'colour', or grey value, of a typeface using such a text. Then one may check how easily readable a text is and how it affects the reader. One may measure how wide or narrow it sets and, upon closer examination, recognize individual letters and their quirks or special features. As one compares typefaces more and more often, one is eventually able to identify and name them.

Of course, this requires attention to detail and practice. This is dummy text. It is not meant to be read for content, but rather to create an even texture in order to evaluate typefaces more easily. One may, at a glance, quickly judge the 'colour', or grey value, of a typeface using such a text. Then one may check how easily readable a text is and

how it affects the reader. One may measure how wide or narrow it sets and, upon closer examination, recognize individual letters and their quirks or special features.

As one compares typefaces more and more often, one is eventually able to identify and name them. Of course, this requires attention to detail and practice. This is dummy text. It is not meant to be read for content, but rather to create an even texture in order to evaluate typefaces more easily. One may, at a glance, quickly judge the 'colour', or grey value, of a typeface using such a text. Then one may check how easily readable a text is and how it affects the reader.

One may measure how wide or narrow it sets and, upon closer examination, recognize individual letters and their quirks or special features. As one compares typefaces more and more often, one is eventually able to identify.

indented paragraph

hyphenation
(end of line break)

column of text

This is dummy text. It is not meant to be read for content, but rather to create an even texture in order to evaluate typefaces more easily. One may, at a glance, quickly judge the 'colour', or grey value, of a typeface using such a text. Then one may check how easily readable a text is and how it affects the reader. One may measure how wide or narrow it sets and, upon closer examination, recognize individual letters and their quirks or special features. As one compares typefaces more and more often, one is eventually able to identify and name them.

Of course, this requires attention to detail and practice. This is dummy text. It is not meant to be read for content, but rather to create an even texture in order to evaluate typefaces more easily. One may, at a glance, quickly judge the 'colour', or grey value, of a typeface using such a text. Then one may check how easily readable a text is and

how it affects the reader. One may measure how wide or narrow it sets and, upon closer examination, recognize individual letters and their quirks or special features.

As one compares typefaces more and more often, one is eventually able to identify and name them. Of course, this requires attention to detail and practice. This is dummy text. It is not meant to be read for content, but rather to create an even texture in order to evaluate typefaces more easily. One may, at a glance, quickly judge the 'colour', or grey value, of a typeface using such a text. Then one may check how easily readable a text is and how it affects the reader.

One may measure how wide or narrow it sets and, upon closer examination, recognize individual letters and their quirks or special features. As one compares typefaces more.

Rivers, found in justified texts, are created due to inconsistency between wordspaces over a number of lines of text.

---

This is dummy text. It is not meant to be read for content, but rather to create an even texture in order to evaluate typefaces more easily. One may, at a glance, quickly judge the 'colour', or grey value, of a typeface using such a text. Then one may check how easily readable a text is and how it affects the reader. One may measure how wide or narrow it sets and, upon closer examination, recognize individual letters and their quirks or special features. As one compares typefaces more and more often, one is eventually able to identify and name them. Of course, this requires attention to detail and practice. This is dummy text. It is not meant to be read for content, but rather to create an even texture in order to evaluate typefaces more easily.
One may, at a glance, quickly judge the 'colour', or grey value, of a typeface using such a text. Then one may check how easily readable a text is and

how it affects the reader.

One may measure how wide or narrow it sets and, upon closer examination, recognize individual letters and their quirks or special features. As one compares typefaces more and more often, one is eventually able to identify and name them. Of course, this requires attention to detail and practice.

This is dummy text. It is not meant to be read for content, but rather to create an even texture in order to evaluate typefaces more easily. One may, at a glance, quickly judge the 'colour', or grey value, of a typeface using such a text. Then one may check how easily readable a text is and how it affects the reader. One may measure how wide or narrow it sets and, upon closer examination, recognize individual letters and their quirks or special features. As one compares typefaces more and more often, one is eventually able to identify.

Widow is the term used to describe a single word of type that is left on its own at the end of a column or paragraph.

An orphan is a short line of type from a column or paragraph left on its own at the top of a new column or page.

# Common mistakes –
# a picture puzzle

Those who argue, 'it's not so important to understand what is meant', would also accept 'youse understands what me means?'

Those who would rather learn to cook well than just produce something edible, need a master chef or at least good cookbooks. Those who wish not only to create adequate typesetting (which *Getting it Right with Type* should serve) but rather 'really good' setting, must deal more thoroughly with the matter.

Attention to detail is the key.

A good sixteen microtypographic errors are hidden in the example on the opposite page. Some of them 'merely' offend the customs of good aesthetics, while others are as bad as broken English.

The search for mistakes is helped overleaf.

THIS IS DUMMY TEXT. Written on the London – Newcastle train. It is not meant to be read for content, but rather to 'create' an even texture in order to evaluate typefaces more easily. One may, at a glance, quickly judge the *colour*, or *grey value*, of a typeface using such a text. Then one may check how easily readable a text is and how it affects the reader. One may measure how wide or narrow it sets and , upon closer examination, recognize individual letters, and their quirks or special features. As one compares typefaces more and more often, one is eventually able to identify and name them... Of course, this requires attention to detail and practice. This is dummy text, written on the London - Newcastle train. It is not meant to be read for content. But rather to create an even texture in order to evaluate typefaces more easily. One may, at a glance, quickly judge the "colour", or grey value, of a typeface using such a text. Then one may check how easily readable a text is and how it affects the reader. One may measure how wide or narrow it sets and, upon closer examination, recognize individual letters and their quirks or special features. As one compares typefaces more and more often, one is eventually able to identify and name them. Of course, this requires attention to detail and practice. This is dummy text, written on the London–Newcastle train. It is not meant to be read for content, but rather to create an even texture in order to evaluate typefaces more easily. One may, at a glance, quickly judge the "colour", or grey value, of a typeface using such a text. . .

# Picture puzzle:
# the solution

THIS IS DUMMY TEXT. Written on the London–Newcastle train. It is not meant to be read for content, but rather to 'create' an even texture in order to evaluate typefaces more easily. One may, at a glance, quickly judge the *colour, or grey value*, of a typeface using such a text. Then one may check how easily readable a text is and how it affects the reader. One may measure how wide or narrow it sets and , upon closer examination, recognize individual letters, and their quirks or special features. As one compares typefaces more and more often, one is eventually able to identify and name them... Of course, this requires attention to detail and practice. This is dummy text, written on the London - Newcastle train. It is not meant to be read for content. But rather to create an even texture in order to evaluate typefaces more easily. One may, at a glance, quickly judge the "colour", or grey value, of a typeface using such a text. Then one may check how easily readable a text is and how it affects the reader. One may measure how wide or narrow it sets and, upon closer examination, recognize individual letters and their quirks or special features. As one compares typefaces more and more often, one is eventually able to identify and name them. Of course, this requires attention to detail and practice. This is dummy text, written on the London – Newcastle train. It is not meant to be read for content, but rather to create an even texture in order to evaluate typefaces more easily. One may, at a glance, quickly judge the "colour", or grey value, of a typeface using such a text. . .

false small capitals

false apostrophe / improper use of foot marks

sloped roman instead of true italic

letterspacing too loose

incorrect placing / spacing of comma

ellipsis too tight

hyphen instead of closed en rule
incorrect use of full point

false quotation marks / improper use of inch marks
letterspacing too tight
ligature not used

inconsistency of typeface

river in justified typesetting
spaced en rule

line justified through letterspacing

ellipsis too loose

# Size of type

When deciding what typesize should be used for a job, consideration should be given to the typeface and its x-height (plus of course the viewer, and where and how it will be read). It is important to understand how a block of text can express a message throught its texture, therefore suiting a particular design solution.

The following examples show six typefaces all set in 10-point but demonstrating different x-heights. It is not the point size but the x-height that determines the visual size.

Helvetica

This is dummy text. It is not meant to be read for content, but rather to create an even texture in order to evaluate typefaces more easily. One may, at a glance, quickly judge the 'colour', or grey value, of a typeface using such a text.

Bembo

This is dummy text. It is not meant to be read for content, but rather to create an even texture in order to evaluate typefaces more easily. One may, at a glance, quickly judge the 'colour', or grey value, of a typeface using such a text.

Meta

This is dummy text. It is not meant to be read for content, but rather to create an even texture in order to evaluate typefaces more easily. One may, at a glance, quickly judge the 'colour', or grey value, of a typeface using such a text.

Bodoni

This is dummy text. It is not meant to be read for content, but rather to create an even texture in order to evaluate typefaces more easily. One may, at a glance, quickly judge the 'colour', or grey value, of a typeface using such a text.

Futura

This is dummy text. It is not meant to be read for content, but rather to create an even texture in order to evaluate typefaces more easily. One may, at a glance, quickly judge the 'colour', or grey value, of a typeface using such a text.

AntiThesis 55

This is dummy text. It is not meant to be read for content, but rather to create an even texture in order to evaluate typefaces more easily. One may, at a glance, quickly judge the 'colour', or grey value, of a typeface using such a text.

The following examples demonstrate that if a large amount of text needs to fit into a small space the designer should select a typeface that has a large x-height but small point size. Condensed typefaces often assist in this case as they allow more characters per line.

New Aster

This is dummy text. It is not meant to be read for content, but rather to create an even texture in order to evaluate typefaces more easily. One may, at a glance, quickly judge the 'colour', or grey value, of a typeface using such a text.

Trade Gothic

This is dummy text. It is not meant to be read for content, but rather to create an even texture in order to evaluate typefaces more easily. One may, at a glance, quickly judge the 'colour', or grey value, of a typeface using such a text.

Avant Garde

This is dummy text. It is not meant to be read for content, but rather to create an even texture in order to evaluate typefaces more easily. One may, at a glance, quickly judge the 'colour', or grey value, of a typeface using such a text.

Century Expanded

This is dummy text. It is not meant to be read for content, but rather to create an even texture in order to evaluate typefaces more easily. One may, at a glance, quickly judge the 'colour', or grey value, of a typeface using such a text.

# Letterspacing

The letterspacing that the designer should employ will vary depending on the typeface that is chosen, whether the type is upper- or lowercase and the amount of text to be set.

### Letterspacing display type
When letterspacing display type the designer must pay particular attention to inconsistency which will be more obvious than letterspacing in text and will be more distracting.

Photosetting style from the 1960s: 'tight, not touching'. Word images are 'spotty'.

Letterspacing

The computer-setting influence: we get into the habit of loose, open word images.

Letterspacing

While it is possible to manipulate word forms, it is important to ensure that the word does not become fragmented.

Letterspacing

A fair word image – no 'spots', no holes.

Letterspacing

## Letterspacing blocks of text

### Tight letterspacing

#### Helvetica

This is dummy text. It is not meant to be read for content, but rather to create an even texture in order to evaluate typefaces more easily. One may, at a glance, quickly judge the 'colour', or grey value, of a typeface using such a text.

#### Bembo

This is dummy text. It is not meant to be read for content, but rather to create an even texture in order to evaluate typefaces more easily. One may, at a glance, quickly judge the 'colour', or grey value, of a typeface using such a text.

#### Frutiger Condensed

This is dummy text. It is not meant to be read for content, but rather to create an even texture in order to evaluate typefaces more easily. One may, at a glance, quickly judge the 'colour', or grey value, of a typeface using such a text.

#### Trade Gothic Extended

This is dummy text. It is not meant to be read for content, but rather to create an even texture in order to evaluate typefaces more easily. One may, at a glance, quickly judge the 'colour', or grey value, of a typeface using such a text.

### Loose letterspacing

#### Helvetica

This is dummy text. It is not meant to be read for content, but rather to create an even texture in order to evaluate typefaces more easily. One may, at a glance, quickly judge the 'colour', or grey value.

#### Bembo

This is dummy text. It is not meant to be read for content, but rather to create an even texture in order to evaluate typefaces more easily. One may, at a glance, quickly judge the 'colour', or grey value, of a typeface.

#### Frutiger Condensed

This is dummy text. It is not meant to be read for content, but rather to create an even texture in order to evaluate typefaces more easily. One may, at a glance, quickly judge the 'colour', or grey value, of a typeface.

#### Trade Gothic Extended

This is dummy text. It is not meant to be read for content, but rather to create an even texture in order to evaluate typefaces more easily. One may, at a glance, quickly judge the 'colour', or grey value.

### Letterspacing and reading

The colour of the printed piece can be affected by letterspacing text. Some caution should be exercised when letterspacing lowercase letterforms as readability can be affected.

This is dummy text. It is not meant to be read for content, but rather to create an even texture in order to evaluate typefaces more easily. One may, at a glance, quickly judge the 'colour', or grey value, of a typeface using such a text. Then one may check how easily readable a text is and how it affects the reader. One may measure how wide or narrow it sets and, upon closer examination, recognize individual letters and their quirks or special features. As one compares

Poor letterspacing with justified type.

This is dummy text. It is not meant to be read for content, but rather to create an even texture in order to evaluate typefaces more easily. One may, at a glance, quickly judge the 'colour', or grey value, of a typeface using such a text. Then one may check how easily readable a text is and how it affects the reader. One may measure how wide or narrow it sets and, upon closer examination, recognize individual letters and their quirks or special features. As one compares

Good letterspacing with justified type
(with hyphenation).

### Letterspacing and meaning

Letterspacing is an emphasizing device. If words are allowed to be spaced out merely in order to satisfy the demands of justification or turn-over, certain words are emphasized without any regard to meaning.

This is dummy text. It is not meant to be read for content, but rather to create an even texture in order to evaluate typefaces more easily. One may, at a glance, quickly judge the 'colour', or grey value, of a typeface using such a text. Then one may check how easily readable a text is and how it affects the reader. One may measure how wide or narrow it sets and, upon closer examination, recognize individual letters and their quirks or special features.

Letterspacing too tight. The overall impression is spotty and uneven.

This is dummy text. It is not meant to be read for content, but rather to create an even texture in order to evaluate typefaces more easily. One may, at a glance, quickly judge the 'colour', or grey value, of a typeface using such a text. Then one may check how easily readable a text is and how it affects the reader. One may measure how wide or narrow it sets and, upon closer examination, recognize individual letters and their quirks or special features.

Well balanced letterspacing. The image is calm and reader friendly.

## Subheads within the text

Typesizes from 14 to 16 point and up (depending on the typeface) should be set with tighter letterspacing. With 'normal' spacing they appear too loose. Wordspacing must also be tightened.

# Letterspacing type over 14 point

This is dummy text. It is not meant to be read for content, but rather to create an even texture in order to evaluate typefaces more easily. One may, at a glance, quickly judge the 'colour', or grey value, of a typeface using such a text.

Subheading with normal letterspacing.

# Letterspacing type over 14 point

This is dummy text. It is not meant to be read for content, but rather to create an even texture in order to evaluate typefaces more easily. One may, at a glance, quickly judge the 'colour', or grey value, of a typeface using such a text.

Subheading with tighter letterspacing.

## Reference sizes

When very small sizes are used, spacing must be loosened. In the following example the type is set in 6 point with normal spacing. Word images appear too tight.

This is dummy text. It is not meant to be read for content, but rather to create an even texture in order to evaluate typefaces more easily. One may, at a glance, quickly judge the 'colour', or grey value, of a typeface using such a text. Then one may check how easily readable a text is and how it affects the reader. One may measure how wide or narrow it sets and, upon closer examination, recognize individual letters and their quirks or special features. As one compares typefaces more and more often, one is eventually able to identify and name them. Of course, this requires attention to detail and practice.

In the next example the same typeface is set more loosely. The text is easier to read. Altering letterspacing belongs to the finer points of typesetting, and it is advisable that you have complete command of what you are doing before venturing into this area.

This is dummy text. It is not meant to be read for content, but rather to create an even texture in order to evaluate typefaces more easily. One may, at a glance, quickly judge the 'colour', or grey value, of a typeface using such a text. Then one may check how easily readable a text is and how it affects the reader. One may measure how wide or narrow it sets and, upon closer examination, recognize individual letters and their quirks or special features. As one compares type-faces more and more often, one is eventually able to identify and name them. Of course, this requires attention to detail and practice.

# Wordspacing

The space between words is termed wordspacing. The same principle that is used in letterspacing also applies to wordspacing; word-spacing has an effect on the overall colour of the text and its readability. The viewer may experience difficulties in reading words that are set too closely together as this can cause problems distinguishing one word from another.

Conversely, words that are set too far apart cause 'rivers' in the text, which disrupt the left-to-right eye movement, as the following examples demonstrate.

This example uses very loose wordspacing, but normal letterspacing.

This is dummy text. It is not meant to be read for content, but rather to create an even texture in order to evaluate typefaces more easily. One may, at a glance, quickly judge the 'colour', or grey value, of a typeface using such a text. Then one may check how easily readable a text is and how it affects the reader. One may measure how wide or narrow it sets and, upon closer examination, recognize individual letters and their quirks or special features. As one compares typefaces more and more often, one is eventually able to identify and name them. Of course, this requires attention to detail and practice.

This example shows normal wordspacing and normal letterspacing.

This is dummy text. It is not meant to be read for content, but rather to create an even texture in order to evaluate typefaces more easily. One may, at a glance, quickly judge the 'colour', or grey value, of a typeface using such a text. Then one may check how easily readable a text is and how it affects the reader. One may measure how wide or narrow it sets and, upon closer examination, recognize individual letters and their quirks or special features. As one compares typefaces more and more often, one is eventually able to identify and name them. Of course, this requires attention to detail and practice.

This is dummy text. It is not meant to be read for content, but rather to create an even texture in order to evaluate typefaces more easily. One may, at a glance, quickly judge the 'colour', or grey value, of a typeface using such a text. Then one may check how easily readable a text is and how it affects the reader. One may measure how wide or narrow it sets and, upon closer examination, recognize individual letters and their quirks or special features. As one compares typefaces more and more often, one is eventually able to identify and name them. Of course, this requires attention to detail and practice.

The final example shows very tight wordspacing, but still with normal letterspacing.

This is dummy text. It is not meant to be read for content, but rather to create an even texture in order to evaluate typefaces more easily. One may, at a glance, quickly judge the 'colour', or grey value, of a typeface using such a text. Then one may check how easily readable a text is and how it affects the reader. One may measure how wide or narrow it sets and, upon closer examination, recognize individual letters and their quirks or special features. As one compares typefaces more and more often, one is eventually able to identify and name them. Of course, this requires attention to detail and practice.

# Leading

Leading is the term used to describe the space between lines of type. It originates from traditional letterpress printing, where the spaces between lines were constructed from strips of lead.

The examples below demonstrate that the space between lines of type is as important as the lines of type themselves. Too little leading can lead to problems with overlapping ascenders and descenders, causing the eye to make unnecessary movements when reading. A large amount of leading creates too much space for the eye to travel between lines. Both cause fatigue when reading lengthy texts.

Preface **v**
Contents **vii**
Rules for setting English **1**
Division of words **14**
Punctuation **38**
References to printed and manuscript sources **50**
Rules for setting foreign languages **87**

10 point type with 10 point leading.

Preface **v**
Contents **vii**
Rules for setting English **1**
Division of words **14**
Punctuation **38**
References to printed and manuscript sources **50**
Rules for setting foreign languages **87**

10 point type with 12 point leading.

Preface **v**
Contents **vii**
Rules for setting English **1**
Division of words **14**
Punctuation **38**
References to printed and manuscript sources **50**
Rules for setting foreign languages **87**

10 point type with 14 point leading.

This is dummy text. It is not meant to be read for content, but rather to create an even texture in order to evaluate typefaces more easily. One may, at a glance, quickly judge the 'colour', or grey value, of a typeface using such a text. Then one may check how easily readable a text is and how it affects the reader.
One may measure how wide or narrow it sets and, upon closer examination, recognize individual letters and their quirks or special features. As one compares typefaces more and more often, one is eventually able to identify and name them. Of course, this requires attention to detail and practice.

An example of tight leading: 10 point type with 10 point leading.

This is dummy text. It is not meant to be read for content, but rather to create an even texture in order to evaluate typefaces more easily. One may, at a glance, quickly judge the 'colour', or grey value, of a typeface using such a text. Then one may check how easily readable a text is and how it affects the reader.
One may measure how wide or narrow it sets and, upon closer examination, recognize individual letters and their quirks or special features. As one compares typefaces more and more often, one is eventually able to identify and name them. Of course, this requires attention to detail and practice.

An example of normal leading: 10 point type with 12 point leading.

This is dummy text. It is not meant to be read for content, but rather to create an even texture in order to evaluate typefaces more easily. One may, at a glance, quickly judge the 'colour', or grey value, of a typeface using such a text. Then one may check how easily readable a text is and how it affects the reader.
One may measure how wide or narrow it sets and, upon closer examination, recognize individual letters and their quirks or special features. As one compares typefaces more and more often, one is eventually able to identify and name them. Of course, this requires attention to detail and practice.

An example of loose leading: 10 point type with 14 point leading.

# Leading
# and wordspacing

The readability of multi-line texts is influenced substantially by the relationship between the leading and the wordspacing. The words in a line must be clearly separate from one another. At the same time, the eye must be prevented from slipping to the wrong line. It is not enough that the eye is merely obediently led along the lines, but rather that one is able to grasp entire areas at once. The typography has to assist with this.

Word space is too large. The eye is not held within the line.

This is dummy text. It is not meant to be read for content, but rather to create an even texture in order to evaluate typefaces more easily. One may, at a glance, quickly judge the 'colour', or grey value, of a typeface.

Word space is too tight. Word images are not adequately separated.

This is dummy text. It is not meant to be read for content, but rather to create an even texture in order to evaluate typefaces more easily. One may, at a glance, quickly judge the 'colour', or grey value, of a typeface.

A well-balanced line. The eye and the brain are not distracted from the content.

This is dummy text. It is not meant to be read for content, but rather to create an even texture in order to evaluate typefaces more easily. One may, at a glance, quickly judge the 'colour', or grey value, of a typeface.

Too large word space. With semi-bold typefaces holes in the lines are especially noticeable.

**This is dummy text. It is not meant to be read for content, but rather to create an even texture in order to evaluate typefaces more easily. One may, at a glance, quickly judge the 'colour', or grey value, of a typeface.**

Here, the 'normal' wordspace is slightly tightened. This aids good line formation.

**This is dummy text. It is not meant to be read for content, but rather to create an even texture in order to evaluate typefaces more easily. One may, at a glance, quickly judge the 'colour', or grey value, of a typeface.**

When a lot of text needs to be accommodated, the largest possible typesize is too often used without enough leading.

This is dummy text. It is not meant to be read for content, but rather to create an even texture in order to evaluate typefaces more easily. One may, at a glance, quickly judge the 'colour', or grey value.

The same typeface, 1½ point sizes smaller, but with the same leading, is more easily readable.

This is dummy text. It is not meant to be read for content, but rather to create an even texture in order to evaluate typefaces more easily. One may, at a glance, quickly judge the 'colour', or grey value, of a typeface using such a text.

Very long lines in a large typesize with no leading. The return trip to the beginning of the next line is made more difficult.

**This is dummy text. It is not meant to be read for content, but rather to create an even texture in order to evaluate typefaces more easily. One may, at a glance, quickly judge the 'colour', or grey value, of a typeface using such a text. Then one may check.**

A small typesize with a large amount of leading. The beginning of the line is found more easily, but with detriment to the texture.

**This is dummy text. It is not meant to be read for content, but rather to create an even texture in order to evaluate typefaces more easily. One may, at a glance, quickly judge the 'colour', or grey value, of a typeface using such a text. Then one may check. how easily readable a text is and how it affects the reader. One may measure how wide or narrow it sets and, upon closer examination, recognize individual letters and their quirks or special features.**

# Line length

As with letterspacing, wordspacing and leading, a line length should be easy to follow. If the line is too long the reader can experience fatigue as the eye has to search for the beginning of each new line (especially if the text is lengthy). If the line is too short words and sentences can be broken too frequently.

This example has a line length
10 characters long.

This is
dummy
text. It is
not
meant to
be read
for
content,
but
rather to
create an
even
texture.

This example has a line length
90 characters long.

This is dummy text. It is not meant to be read for content, but rather to create an even texture in order to evaluate typefaces more easily. One may, at a glance, quickly judge the 'colour', or grey value, of a typeface using such a text. Then one may check how easily readable a text is and how it affects the reader. One may measure how wide or narrow it sets and, upon closer examination, recognize individual letters and their quirks or special features. As one compares typefaces more and more often, one is eventually able to identify and name them. Of course, this requires attention to detail and practice.

# Leading and line length

Recognize this situation? Just before going to sleep you decide to do a bit of reading. End of the line – beginning of the line. Hey, I've just read that! When it happens again you put the book down. This is often due to inadequate leading. The examples below and on the following page show different column widths and leading but use the same typeface.

This is dummy text. It is not meant to be read for content, but rather to create an even texture in order to evaluate typefaces more easily. One may, at a glance, quickly judge the 'colour', or grey value, of a typeface using such a text.

This is dummy text. It is not meant to be read for content, but rather to create an even texture in order to evaluate typefaces more easily. One may, at a glance, quickly judge the 'colour', or grey value, of a typeface using such a text. Then one may check how easily readable a text is and how it affects the reader. One may measure how wide or narrow it sets and, upon closer examination, recognize individual letters and their quirks or special features. As one compares typefaces more and more often, one is eventually able to identify and name them.

This is dummy text. It is not meant to be read for content, but rather to create an even texture in order to evaluate typefaces more easily. One may, at a glance, quickly judge the 'colour', or grey value, of a typeface using such a text.

This is dummy text. It is not meant to be read for content, but rather to create an even texture in order to evaluate typefaces more easily. One may, at a glance, quickly judge the 'colour', or grey value, of a typeface using such a text. Then one may check how easily readable a text is and how it affects the reader. One may measure how wide or narrow it sets and, upon closer examination, recognize individual letters and their quirks or special features. As one compares typefaces more and more often, one is eventually able to identify and name them.

This is dummy text. It is not meant to be read for content, but rather to create an even texture in order to evaluate typefaces more easily. One may, at a glance, quickly judge the 'colour', or grey value, of a typeface using such a text.

This is dummy text. It is not meant to be read for content, but rather to create an even texture in order to evaluate typefaces more easily. One may, at a glance, quickly judge the 'colour', or grey value, of a typeface using such a text. Then one may check how easily readable a text is and how it affects the reader. One may measure how wide or narrow it sets and, upon closer examination, recognize individual letters and their quirks or special features. As one compares typefaces more and more often, one is eventually able to identify and name them.

The examples on pages 83 and 84 clearly show that one cannot say, 'this type-face needs 12-point leading'. It depends on the line length. For these examples, we chose an especially tricky typeface. The thick vertical strokes tend to guide the eye between lines when reading; it is therefore the job of the leading to ensure that the eye stays within the line. Note: the longer the line, the larger the leading needs to be. The shorter the line, the less leading is needed.

This is dummy text. It is not meant to be read for content, but rather to create an even texture in order to evaluate typefaces more easily. One may, at a glance, quickly judge the 'colour', or grey value, of a typeface using such a text. Then one may check how easily read-able a text is and how it affects the reader. One may measure how wide or narrow it sets and, upon closer examination, recognize individual letters and their quirks or special features. As one compares typefaces more and more often, one is eventually able to identify and name them. This is dummy text. It is not meant to be read for content, but rather to create an even texture in order to evaluate typefaces more easily. One may, at a glance, quickly judge the 'colour', or grey value, of a typeface using such a text.

This is dummy text. It is not meant to be read for content, but rather to create an even texture in order to evaluate typefaces more easily. One may, at a glance, quickly judge the 'colour', or grey value, of a typeface using such a text. Then one may check how easily read-able a text is and how it affects the reader. One may measure how wide or narrow it sets and, upon closer examination, recognize individual letters and their quirks or special features. As one compares typefaces more and more often, one is eventually able to identify and name them. This is dummy text. It is not meant to be read for content, but rather to create an even texture in order to evaluate typefaces more easily. One may, at a glance, quickly judge the 'colour', or grey value, of a typeface using such a text.

This is dummy text. It is not meant to be read for content, but rather to create an even texture in order to evaluate typefaces more easily. One may, at a glance, quickly judge the 'colour', or grey value, of a typeface using such a text. Then one may check how easily read-able a text is and how it affects the reader. One may measure how wide or narrow it sets and, upon closer examination, recognize individual letters and their quirks or special features. As one compares typefaces more and more often, one is eventually able to identify and name them. This is dummy text. It is not meant to be read for content, but rather to create an even texture in order to evaluate typefaces more easily. One may, at a glance, quickly judge the 'colour', or grey value, of a typeface using such a text.

# Alignment
# of text

The examples in this section demonstrate the four main ways of aligning text: ranged left, ranged right, justified and centred, and the particular aspects that should be considered when each is used. As with all other aspects of typography, when deciding how to align text, consideration should be given to the function of the communication. What is the author trying to say and how should this be communicated?

### Ranged left

With this alignment word spaces are equal in all lines, giving a calm inner structure. This type of setting, also called flush-left or ragged-right, necessarily results in lines of unequal length.

This is dummy text. It is not meant to be read for content, but rather to create an even texture in order to evaluate typefaces more easily. One may, at a glance, quickly judge the 'colour', or grey value, of a typeface using such a text. Then one may check how easily readable a text is and how it affects the reader. One may measure how wide or narrow it sets and, upon closer examination, recognize individual letters and their quirks or special features. As one compares typefaces more and more often, one is eventually able to identify and name them.

One should not just let the computer decide where and when lines are broken. This example shows bad ragged setting with misleading hyphenations and an irregular hyphenation zone.

This is dummy text. It is not meant to be read for content, but rather to create an even texture in order to evaluate typefaces more easily. One may, at a glance, quickly judge the 'colour', or grey value, of a typeface using such a text. Then one may check how easily readable a text is and how it affects the reader. One may measure how wide or narrow it sets and, upon closer examination, recognize individual letters and their quirks or special features. As one compares typefaces more and more often, one is eventually able.

The same text in reworked ranged-left setting. Line breaks are revised in terms of sense as well as aesthetics.

This is dummy text. It is not meant to be read for content, but rather to create an even texture in order to evaluate typefaces more easily. One may, at a glance, quickly judge the 'colour', or grey value, of a typeface using such a text. Then one may check how easily readable a text is and how it affects the reader. One may measure how wide or narrow it sets and, upon closer examination, recognize individual letters and their quirks or special features. As one compares typefaces more and more often, one is eventually able.

This is dummy text. It is not meant to be read for content, but rather to create an even texture in order to evaluate typefaces more easily. One may, at a glance, quickly judge the 'colour', or grey value, of a typeface using such a text. Then one may check how easily readable a text is and how it affects the reader. One may measure how wide or narrow it sets and, upon closer examination, recognize individual letters and their quirks or special features. As one compares typefaces more and more often, one is eventually able to identify and name them. Of course, this requires attention to detail and practice.

**Ranged right**
A sometimes aesthetically interesting method of setting, also called flush-right or ragged-left, to which, however, the text often reacts gingerly. Words and word fragments stand out to the left, accentuating the chance line breaks. This is a useful format to use as a caption alongside an image. However, the eye focuses on the end of the line rather than the beginning, so it probably should not be used for lengthy texts.

This is dummy text. It is not meant to be read for content, but rather to create an even texture in order to evaluate typefaces more easily. One may, at a glance, quickly judge the 'colour', or grey value, of a typeface using such a text. Then one may check how easily readable a text is and how it affects the reader. One may measure how wide or narrow it sets and, upon closer examination, recognize individual letters and their quirks or special features. As one compares typefaces more and more often, one is eventually able to identify and name them. Of course, this requires attention to detail and practice.

**Justified**
This format is used most commonly within newspapers, magazines and books where text has the same line length, with lines flush left and right. Consequently, word-spacing is adjusted and will differ between lines, causing rivers of adjacent white spaces to run through the text. The designer can reduce this problem by careful adjustment of line breaks and use of hyphenation.

This is dummy text. It is not meant to be read for content, but rather to create an even texture in order to evaluate typefaces more easily. One may, at a glance, quickly judge the 'colour', or grey value, of a typeface using such a text. Then one may check how easily readable a text is and how it affects the reader. One may measure how wide or narrow it sets and, upon closer examination, recognize individual letters and their quirks or special features. As one compares typefaces more and more often, one is eventually able to identify and name them. Of course, this requires attention to detail and practice.

This example demonstrates that a few hyphenated lines are less disturbing than 'holey' ones. (When avoiding rivers it is acceptable to have no more than two consecutive line-end hyphens.) Sensible hyphenations are difficult to manage in justified setting – the voids impede easy reading.

This is dummy text. It is not meant to be read for content, but rather to create an even texture in order to evaluate typefaces more easily. One may, at a glance, quickly judge the 'colour', or grey value, of a typeface using such a text. Then one may check how easily readable a text is and how it affects the reader. One may measure how wide or narrow it sets and, upon closer examination, recognize individual letters and their quirks or special features.

Narrow justified setting leads to unavoidable bad 'holey' composition. With larger column widths, aesthetics take precedence over functionality when it comes to deciding whether to set justified or ragged.

This is dummy text. It is not meant to be
read for content, but rather to create an even texture
in order to evaluate typefaces more easily.
One may, at a glance, quickly judge the 'colour',
or grey value, of a typeface using such a text.
Then one may check how easily readable a text is and
how it affects the reader.
One may measure how wide or narrow it sets
and, upon closer examination, recognize individual
letters and their quirks or special features.
As one compares typefaces more and more often, one
is eventually able to identify and name them.
Of course, this requires attention to
detail and practice.

**Centred**
In this setting both the beginnings
and the ends of the lines are
ragged. The lines have equal
weight due to the symmetry.
The designer must control the line
breaks so the shape of the text
does not appear jagged but has an
interesting silhouette.

This is dummy text. It is not meant to be read for
content, but rather to create an even texture in order
to evaluate typefaces more easily. One may, at a glance,
quickly judge the 'colour', or grey value, of a typeface
using such a text. Then one may check how
easily readable a text is and how it affects the reader.
One may measure how wide or narrow it sets
and, upon closer examination, recognize individual
letters and their quirks or special features. As one
compares typefaces more and more often, one is
eventually able to identify and name them. Of course,
this requires attention to detail and practice.

This example shows the same text
centred, where the overall shape
is unpleasing.

# Line endings: justification

Line endings establish the point in the sentence where reading is interrupted, and most of the time the reader hardly notices. However, there are cases when using justified text in which the sense of the text, rather than the column measure, should decide where line endings should occur. In these cases, you should not trust the hyphenation program on the computer but instead read the text and decide for yourself.

These examples based on real-life graphics demonstrate that some designers do not pay enough attention to where sensible line breaks should occur.

**a.** Hier haben wir eine Reise mit einem kleinen Picknick in der Taiga. **b.** Hier haben wir eine Reise mit einem kleinen Einkaufstrip in Hongkong. **c.** Hier haben wir eine Reise mit einer interessanten Stadtrundfahrt in Berlin. **d.** Hier haben wir eine Reise mit einer langen Dampferfahrt auf dem Rhein. **e.** Hier haben wir eine Reise mit einem tollen Ausflug zum Fudschijama. **f.** Hier haben wir eine Reise mit einer teuren Fotosafari in Afrika.

| | |
|---|---|
| PRINCIPLES OF PILATES | 10 |
| The benefits of pil-ates | 12 |
| Physiology | 23 |
| Posture and breath-ing | 30 |

AN INSTRUMENT IS A COMPANION

Me and my old Chevy have seen a lot of the country together.

Q: Who's gonna stop me?
A: Me and old Betsy here [said by the cowboy reaching for his gun].

## 19 HOW TO USE MUSIC AND THE ARTS

**GRANT APPLICATION:** Money was available from the Woodland Trust's Community Woodland Network towards the costs of training tools and promotion. It was agreed to apply for funding, noting that the closing date was July 30. Mr Bawden and Mr Squire to complete the application form after the meeting.

In the following cases we may apply the rule that almost-full lines should not be stretched out to the full column width.

Use ranged left (or right) setting when dealing with:

Bad

Good

**Line endings and typo-graphy**
This is dummy text. It is not meant to be read for content, but rather to create an even texture in order to more easily evaluate typefaces.

**Line endings and typography**
This is dummy text. It is not meant to be read for content, but rather to create an even texture in order to more easily evaluate typefaces.

• titles and subtitles

• tables of contents (in the good example page numbers have also been ranged left, see also p.124)

– Discuss the known setting meth-ods
– Write 1000 times: I will set ranged left

– Discuss the known setting methods
– Write 1000 times:
I will set ranged left

• assignments in text books

Duane Hanson, *More than Reality*, Hantje Cantz Publishers, Ostfildern-Ruit, 2001
Nicolas Barker, *The Oxford University Press and the Spread of Learning 1478–1978, An Illustrated History*, 2 volumes. Oxford, Clarendon Press, 1978

Duane Hanson, *More than Reality*, Hantje Cantz Publishers, Ostfildern-Ruit, 2001
Nicolas Barker, *The Oxford University Press and the Spread of Learning 1478–1978, An Illustrated History*, 2 volumes, Oxford, Clarendon Press, 1978

• In bibliographies and similar lists, with many abbreviations and dates, justified setting creates disastrous holes. Given names are separated from family names, months from their years, etc. Only good ranged left (or right) setting can help.

# Line endings:
# widows and orphans

Widows and orphans disrupt reading. The colour and texture of the text is broken, as is the visuality of the layout. To combat widows and orphans the designer should concentrate on the line endings and break them accordingly.

To avoid widows the designer can either edit the copy so that the text ends on the previous line, or bring text down to accompany the widow, taking care to avoid hyphenations and poor line breaks.

To avoid orphans the designer can edit the copy so that text ends at the end of the column or page. Alternatively, the designer can carefully tighten the word spacing by kerning within the paragraph to pull the text back or expand to enable a more substantial amount of text to be at the top of the new column or page.

Incorrect.

Correct.

# Paragraphs

The beginning of a new paragraph can be indicated in a number of ways. Paragraphs may be indicated by a line space or indentation. In medieval manuscripts, where text ran continuously, a pilcrow (¶) was used.

## Space between paragraphs

Paragraphs can be separated by a line space, which ensures that within a layout typography across columns will align. This space can be specified, which gives the designer more control.

This is dummy text. It is not meant to be read for content, but rather to create an even texture in order to evaluate typefaces more easily. One may, at a glance, quickly judge the 'colour', or grey value, of a typeface using such a text. Then one may check how easily readable a text is and how it affects the reader.

One may measure how wide or narrow it sets and, upon closer examination, recognize individual letters and their quirks or special features. As one compares typefaces more and more often, one is eventually able to identify and name them.

Of course, this requires attention to detail and practice. This is dummy text. It is not meant to be read for content, but rather to create an even texture in order to evaluate typefaces more easily. One may, at a glance, quickly judge the 'colour', or grey value, of a typeface using such a text. Then one may check how easily readable a text is and how it affects the reader. One may measure how wide or narrow it sets and, upon closer examination, recognize individual letters and their quirks or special features.

As one compares typefaces more and more often, one is eventually able to identify and name them. Of course, this requires attention to detail and practice. This is dummy text. It is not meant to be read for content, but rather to create an even texture in order to evaluate typefaces more easily.

## New line

The start of the paragraph is indicated by starting a new line with no indents and no spaces. Readability can be a problem as the eye has to differentiate between sentences and paragraphs. Sentences that happen to fall at the beginning of the line can be mistaken for a paragraph.

This is dummy text. It is not meant to be read for content, but rather to create an even texture in order to evaluate typefaces more easily. One may, at a glance, quickly judge the 'colour', or grey value, of a typeface using such a text. Then one may check how easily readable a text is and how it affects the reader.
One may measure how wide or narrow it sets and, upon closer examination, recognize individual letters and their quirks or special features. As one compares typefaces more and more often, one is eventually able to identify and name them.
Of course, this requires attention to detail and practice. This is dummy text. It is not meant to be read for content, but rather to create an even texture in order to evaluate typefaces more easily. One may, at a glance, quickly judge the 'colour', or grey value, of a typeface using such a text. Then one may check how easily readable a text is and how it affects the reader. One may measure how wide or narrow it sets and, upon closer examination, recognize individual letters and their quirks or special features.
As one compares typefaces more and more often, one is eventually able to identify and name them. Of course, this requires attention to detail and practice. This is dummy text. It is not meant to be read for content, but rather to create an even texture in order to evaluate typefaces more easily. One may, at a glance, quickly judge the 'colour', or grey value, of a typeface using such a text. Then one may check how easily readable a text is and how it affects the reader.

## Indentation

Indentation is a traditional method of indicating paragraphs. Usually the indent is the same size as the leading or the size of type.

## Hanging indent

All the lines are indented except for the first line of the paragraph, which is set to the full measure. Note that if the paragraph that uses either indentation or a hanging indent begins with a quote mark the indent will need to be reduced in width so that it will visually appear the same as the others.

This is dummy text. It is not meant to be read for content, but rather to create an even texture in order to evaluate typefaces more easily. One may, at a glance, quickly judge the 'colour', or grey value, of a typeface using such a text. Then one may check how easily readable a text is and how it affects the reader.

One may measure how wide or narrow it sets and, upon closer examination, recognize individual letters and their quirks or special features. As one compares typefaces more and more often, one is eventually able to identify and name them.

Of course, this requires attention to detail and practice. This is dummy text. It is not meant to be read for content, but rather to create an even texture in order to evaluate typefaces more easily. One may, at a glance, quickly judge the 'colour', or grey value, of a typeface using such a text. Then one may check how easily readable a text is and how it affects the reader. One may measure how wide or narrow it sets and, upon closer examination, recognize individual letters and their quirks or special features.

As one compares typefaces more and more often, one is eventually able to identify and name them. Of course, this requires attention to detail and practice. This is dummy text. It is not meant to be read for content, but rather to create an even texture in order to evaluate typefaces more easily. One may, at a glance, quickly judge the 'colour', or grey value, of a typeface using such a text. Then one may check how easily readable a text is and how it affects the reader.

This is dummy text. It is not meant to be read for content, but rather to create an even texture in order to evaluate typefaces more easily. One may, at a glance, quickly judge the 'colour', or grey value, of a typeface using such a text. Then one may check how easily readable a text is and how it affects the reader. One may measure how wide or narrow it sets and, upon closer examination, recognize individual letters and their quirks or special features.

As one compares typefaces more and more often, one is eventually able to identify and name them. Of course, this requires attention to detail and practice. This is dummy text.

It is not meant to be read for content, but rather to create an even texture in order to evaluate typefaces more easily. One may, at a glance, quickly judge the 'colour', or grey value, of a typeface using such a text. Then one may check how easily readable a text is and how it affects the reader.

One may measure how wide or narrow it sets and, upon closer examination, recognize individual letters and their quirks or special features. As one compares typefaces more and more often, one is eventually able to identify and name them. Of course, this requires attention to detail and practice.

This is dummy text. It is not meant to be read for content, but rather to create an even texture in order to evaluate typefaces more easily. One may, at a glance, quickly judge the 'colour', or grey value, of a typeface using such a text.

# Text in boxes /
# boxes in text

## Text in boxes

Boxes demarcated by rules and coloured or tinted backgrounds are widely used by designers within a variety of media such as websites, books or magazines.

Whether – as is surely intended – they attract attention and promote reading can be for the moment set to one side. In any case, the type-face must be strong enough to cope with the background and the background must be light enough not to overwhelm the type.

This is a bad example. The type area and the background area should, in most cases, not be equal in size. The background does not frame the text and therefore does not assist the reader with a margin.

This is dummy text. It is not meant to be read for content, but rather to create an even texture in order to evaluate typefaces more easily. One may, at a glance, quickly judge the 'colour', or grey value, of a typeface using such a text. Then one may check how easily readable a text is and how it affects the reader. One may measure how wide or narrow it sets and, upon closer examination, recognize individual letters and their quirks or special features. As one compares typefaces more and more often, one is eventually able to identify and name them. Of course, this requires attention to detail and practice. This is dummy text. It is not meant to be read for content, but rather to create an even texture in order to evaluate typefaces more easily. One may, at a glance, quickly judge the 'colour'.

With a ruled frame, a white margin is left around the type.

This is dummy text. It is not meant to be read for content, but rather to create an even texture in order to evaluate typefaces more easily. One may, at a glance, quickly judge the 'colour', or grey value, of a typeface using such a text. Then one may check how easily readable a text is and how it affects the reader. One may measure how wide or narrow it sets and, upon closer examination, recognize individual letters and their quirks or special features. As one compares typefaces more and more often, one is eventually able to identify and name them. Of course, this requires attention to detail and practice.

A coloured or tinted area must be sized as though it had a ruled border.

This is dummy text. It is not meant to be read for content, but rather to create an even texture in order to evaluate typefaces more easily. One may, at a glance, quickly judge the 'colour', or grey value, of a typeface using such a text. Then one may check how easily readable a text is and how it affects the reader. One may measure how wide or narrow it sets and, upon closer examination, recognize individual letters and their quirks or special features. As one compares typefaces more and more often, one is eventually able to identify and name them. Of course, this requires attention to detail and practice.

The same coloured or tinted area with a ruled border.

This is dummy text. It is not meant to be read for content, but rather to create an even texture in order to evaluate typefaces more easily. One may, at a glance, quickly judge the 'colour', or grey value, of a typeface using such a text. Then one may check how easily readable a text is and how it affects the reader. One may measure how wide or narrow it sets and, upon closer examination, recognize individual letters and their quirks or special features. As one compares typefaces more and more often, one is eventually able to identify and name them. Of course, this requires attention to detail and practice.

## Boxes in text

Since columns of text can be seen as unfriendly, small text excerpts, or 'call-outs' are inserted in the columns of many magazines, as well as photographs, illustrations and design motifs. Runaround is the term used when text is diverted around these elements (as shown here), which naturally breaks the block effect of the text columns.

These three examples should serve to demonstrate that one may arrive at attractive results using simple methods rather than complicated effects.

Follow this rule of thumb. Type in a box is almost always set too low. It appears to be sliding downwards. The area above the type should be optically slightly smaller than that below. This applies also to coloured or bordered backgrounds.

This is dummy text. It is not meant to be read for content, but rather to create an even texture in order to evaluate typefaces more easily. One may, at a glance, quickly judge the 'colour', or grey value, of a typeface using such a text. Then one may check how easily readable a text is and how it affects the reader. One may measure how wide or narrow it sets and, upon closer examination, recognize individual letters and their quirks or special features. As one compares typefaces more and more often, one is eventually able to identify and name them. Of course, this requires attention to detail and practice. This is dummy text. It is not meant to be read for content, but rather to create an even texture in order to evaluate typefaces more easily. One may, at a glance, quickly judge the 'colour', or grey value, of a typeface using such a text. Then one may check how easily readable a text is and how it affects the reader. One may measure how wide or narrow it sets and, upon closer examination, recognize individual letters and their quirks or special features. As one compares typefaces more and more often, one is eventually able to identify and name them. Of course, this requires attention to detail and practice. This is dummy text. It is not meant to be read for content, but rather to create an even texture in

**text in boxes**

This is dummy text. It is not meant to be read for content, but rather to create an even texture in order to evaluate typefaces more easily. One may, at a glance, quickly judge the 'colour', or grey value, of a typeface using such a text. Then one may check how easily readable a text is and how it affects the reader. One may measure how wide or narrow it sets and, upon closer examination, recognize individual letters and their quirks or special features. As one compares typefaces more and more often, one is eventually able to identify and name them. Of course, this requires attention to detail and practice. This is dummy text. It is not meant to be read for content, but rather to create an even texture in order to evaluate typefaces more easily. One may, at a glance, quickly judge the 'colour', or grey value, of a typeface using such a text. Then one may check how easily readable a text is and how it affects the reader. One may measure how wide or narrow it sets and, upon closer examination, recognize individual letters and their quirks or special features. As one compares typefaces more and more often, one is eventually able to identify and name them. Of course, this requires attention to detail and practice. This is dummy text. It is not meant to be read for content, but rather to create an even texture in

**text in boxes**

This is dummy text. It is not meant to be read for content, but rather to create an even texture in order to evaluate typefaces more easily. One may, at a glance, quickly judge the 'colour', or grey value, of a typeface using such a text. Then one may check how easily readable a text is and how it affects the reader. One may measure how wide or narrow it sets and, upon closer examination, recognize individual letters and their quirks or special features. As one compares typefaces more and more often, one is eventually able to identify and name them. Of course, this requires attention to detail and practice. This is dummy text. It is not meant to be read for content, but rather to create an even texture in order to evaluate typefaces more easily. One may, at a glance, quickly judge the 'colour', or grey value, of a typeface using such a text. Then one may check how easily readable a text is and how it affects the reader. One may measure how wide or narrow it sets and, upon closer examination, recognize individual letters and their quirks or special features. As one compares typefaces more and more often, one is eventually able to identify and name them. Of course, this requires attention to detail and practice. This is dummy text. It is not meant to be read for content, but rather to create an even texture in

**text in boxes**

# 3

# Layout

## Grids and text

Covering:
The grid: technical terminology
Text hierarchy
Page layout
Text and image
Footnotes, bibliographies, contents, indexes
Tabular information

# Typography
# and layout

There are some designers who establish their designs to which everything must submit: texts must be shortened and images cropped, whether it suits the content or not. In fact, it should be the other way around: text and images determine the typography and the layout. It is essential to establish a clear relationship between text and images as they should not be observed individually, but complement each other.

The two previous chapters have introduced you to letterforms, typefaces, words and paragraphs. This chapter will introduce you to the basics of layout design using grids, enabling you to put some of your newly acquired typographic knowledge into practice for a particular purpose. There are many rules that can be adopted within this chapter. It is of course vital to observe these but it is also important to consider that in some circumstances these rules can be broken.

To produce typographically resolved and compositionally balanced designs the type user should consider:

- a grid system
- columns within layout
- choice of typeface
- ligatures
- hierarchy of information
- title treatments
- subheading treatments
- italics used within text
- captions
- alignment of text (ranged left, ranged right, justified, centred)
- text–image relationships
- tabular work

These real-life examples illustrate design that serves its purpose. Well-considered typography, demonstrating a clear logical hierarchy and complemented by an intelligent use of images, is a prerequisite for successful layout.

Phil Baines, Penguin book jacket: *Great Ideas* series 2, *Marco Polo.*

Spread from Lucienne Roberts and Julia Thrift, *The Designer and the Grid.*

Vince Frost, spread from *Big* magazine.

A page from *The Guardian* newspaper.

Vince Frost, spread from *Big* magazine.

# The grid:
# technical terminology

## The grid

When designing a layout and working with text and / or images the use of a grid is essential, as it is the basis on which information is organized and clarified, ensuring legibility. The grid provides a framework where text, image and space can be combined in a unified and cohesive manner.

A grid is a structure made up of horizontal and vertical lines, and on it the designer places components such as headings, text, images, captions etc. The grid can be as complex or simple as the designer needs. It is used to express the information in a sequential and logical manner, so that readers can easily navigate their way through the page. Grids are used within a variety of formats, from posters to websites. In a magazine or book design the grid is constructed as a double-page spread.

This example shows a grid where the proportions of the text area are established from the shape of the page, i.e. the height of the text area is the same as the width of the full page. Note that the text area will always remain the same, regardless of the scale of the page.

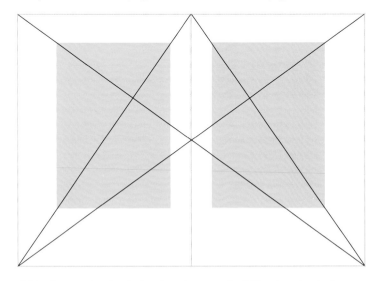

Grids often need to be designed to give more flexibility than the single column of text per page. This is due to a change in our reading patterns. Although we still read consecutively, our attention is drawn to both magazines and coffee table books which are often larger in format and highly illustrated. The grid structures for these formats have to accommodate a greater variety of material such as photographs, illustrations, headings, captions, references, charts; they need to be more complicated than for a grid using only text and may utilize more modules. Therefore, the design of the grid has to be relevant to its purpose.

The golden section has been used for centuries. The Greeks used the golden section to establish balance in the design of architecture, for example the Parthenon, and it was re-discovered by artists and architects during the Renaissance period.

Note: the grid is the underlying structure on which the information is positioned and presented. With regard to typography it is essential to consider the following in conjunction with designing a grid: choice of typeface, size of type, type style (bold, italic, condensed etc), letterspacing, wordspacing, leading, paragraph spacing, kerning, all of which have been covered in chapters 1 and 2.

The golden section is constructed through mathematical calculation: the ratio being 1:1.61803. The example below (steps one to four) demonstrates its construction from a simple square. Step four indicates the proportions of the golden section.

The Fibonacci sequence is a mathematical series discovered in the 12th century by Leonardo Fibonacci and is used to establish proportion. The sequence of numbers below demonstrate that the sum of two numbers establishes the next number, for example (2+3) 5.
0 (0+1) 1 (1+1) 2 (1+2) 3 (2+3) 5 (3+5) 8 (5+8) 13...

The ratio of each successive pair of numbers approximates 1.618, the same as the golden section.

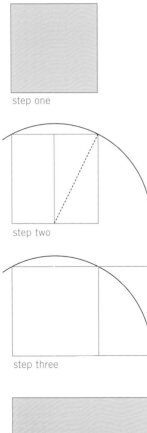

step one

step two

step three

step four

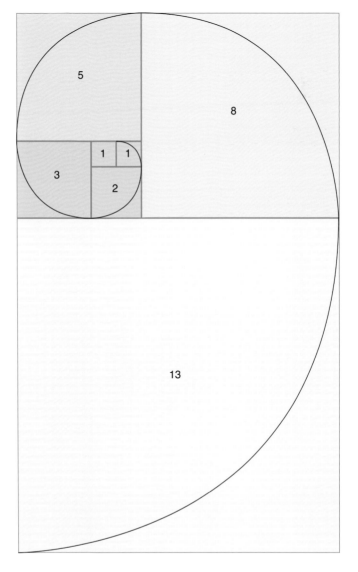

The following examples demonstrate the terminology used when designing spreads.

The left-hand page.
Text area. This example indicates the text area, the area that accommodates the text.

The right-hand page.
Margins. The area that is not accommodated by the text.

The left-hand page.
Horizontal and vertical gutters. These are the inner margins of the page that separate modules from one another.

The right hand page.
Module (or field). An area calculated in depth by the text leading and width by the text line length.

This is dummy text. It is not meant to be read for content, but rather to create an even texture in order to evaluate typefaces more easily. One may, at a glance, quickly judge the 'colour', or grey value, of a typeface using such a text. Then one may check how easily readable a text is and how it affects the reader. One may measure how wide or narrow it sets and, upon closer examination, recognize individual letters and their quirks or special features. As one compares typefaces more and more often, one is eventually able to identify and name them.

Of course, this requires attention to detail and practice. This is dummy text. It is not meant to be read for content, but rather to create an even texture in order to evaluate typefaces more easily. One may, at a glance, quickly judge the 'colour', or grey value, of a typeface using such a text. Then one may check how easily readable a text is and how it affects the reader. One may measure how wide or narrow it sets and, upon closer examination, recognize individual letters and their quirks or special features.

As one compares typefaces more and more often, one is eventually able to identify and name them. Of course, this requires attention to detail and practice. This is dummy text. It is not meant to be read for content, but rather to create an even texture in order to evaluate typefaces more easily. One may, at a glance, quickly judge the 'colour', or grey value, of a typeface using such a text.

Then one may check how easily readable a text is and how it affects the reader. One may measure how wide or narrow it sets and, upon closer examination, recognize individual letters and their quirks or special features.

Passive and active corners. The active corner (the strongest) is the top left module, whilst the passive corner (the weakest) is the bottom right module.

The left-hand page.
Folio or page number.
Even numbers are always positioned on the left-hand page (verso), odd numbers on the right-hand page (recto).

The right-hand page.
Running head and running foot. These list chapter titles and section headings to indicate to readers where they are within a book or magazine. A running head is situated above the text, a running foot below. Only one or the other is used.

# Columns
# and layout

When layouts for books or magazines are designed, text is positioned on the grid within columns, which are formed by modules, allowing for more than one module or column per page. Using columns enables the designer to maintain consistent line length.

Before a layout and number of columns can be established for a printed work it is essential to consider the following:

• How many pages will there be?

• What is the page size?

• Is the publication text-heavy or image-heavy?

• What is the optimum line length for the text? (This will establish the column width.)

• What leading will be used? (This will establish the column depth.)

• What will the binding be like?

The following examples look at a range of vertical and horizontal layouts with columns.

3-column grid.

5-column grid. This format enables the designer to accommodate text over all five modules. Here the designer uses two modules to create a column (resulting in two columns over four modules), leaving a narrower column (module area) for secondary information, such as captions.

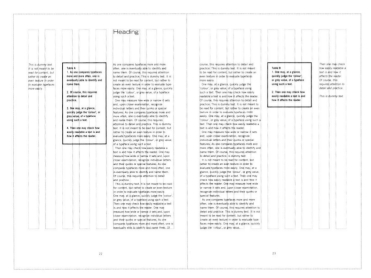

6-column grid. This format is similar to the 5-column grid; however it allows for a wider module area for the secondary information.

9-column grid.

## Heading

This is dummy text. It is not meant to be read for content, but rather to create an even texture in order to evaluate typefaces more easily. One may, at a glance, quickly judge the 'colour', or grey value, of a typeface using such a text. Then one may check how easily readable a text is and how it affects the reader. One may measure how wide or narrow it sets and, upon closer examination, recognize individual letters and their quirks or special features. As one compares typefaces more and more often, one is eventually able to identify and name them. Of course, this requires attention to detail and practice. This is dummy text.

It is not meant to be read for content, but rather to create an even texture in order to evaluate typefaces more easily. One may, at a glance, quickly judge the 'colour', or grey value, of a typeface using such a text. Then one may check how easily readable a text is and how it affects the reader. One may measure how wide

or narrow it sets and, upon closer examination, recognize individual letters and their quirks or special features. As one compares typefaces more and more often, one is eventually able to identify and name them. Of course, this requires attention to detail and practice. This is dummy text.

It is not meant to be read for content, but rather to create an even texture in order to evaluate typefaces more easily. One may, at a glance, quickly judge the 'colour', or grey value, of a typeface using such a text. Then one may check how easily readable a text is and how it affects the reader. One may measure how wide or narrow it sets and, upon closer examination, recognize individual letters and their quirks or special features. As one compares typefaces more and more often, one is eventually able to identify and name them. Of course, this requires attention to detail and practice. This is dummy text. It is not meant to be read

for content, but rather to create an even texture in order to evaluate typefaces more easily.

One may, at a glance, quickly judge the 'colour', or grey value, of a typeface using such a text. Then one may check how easily readable a text is and how it affects the reader. Of course, this requires attention to detail and practice. This is dummy text. It is not meant to be read for content, but rather to reate an even texture in order to evaluate typefaces more easily.

One may, at a glance, quickly judge the 'colour', or grey value, of a typeface using such a text. Then one may check how easily readable a text is and how it affects the reader. One may measure how wide or narrow it sets and, upon closer examination, recognize individual letters and their quirks or special features. As one compares typefaces more and more often, one is eventually able to identify and name them. Of course, this requires attention to detail and practice. This

dummy text. It is not meant to be read for content, but rather to create an even texture in order to evaluate typefaces more easily. One may, at a glance, quickly judge the 'colour', or grey value, of a typeface using such a text.

Then one may check how easily readable a text is and how it affects the reader. One may measure how wide or narrow it sets and, upon closer examination, recognize individual letters and their quirks or special features.

As one compares typefaces more and more often, one is eventually able to identify and name them.

Of course, this requires attention to detail and practice. This is dummy text. It is not meant to be read for content, but rather to create an even texture in order to evaluate typefaces more easily. One may, at a glance, quickly judge the 'colour', or of a typeface using such a text. Then one may check how

2-column grid. There can be a problem with the 2-column grid. If the gutter is too large, the eye gets drawn to the gutter rather than to the text. The 3-column grid overcomes this problem.

## Heading

This is dummy text. It is not meant to be read for content, but rather to create an even texture in order to evaluate typefaces more easily. One may, at a glance, quickly judge the 'colour', or grey value, of a typeface using such a text. Then one may check how easily readable a text is and how it affects the reader.

One may measure how wide or narrow it sets and, upon closer examination, recognize individual letters and their quirks or special features. As one compares typefaces more and more often, one is eventually able to identify and name them. Of course, this

requires attention to detail and practice. This is dummy text.

It is not meant to be read for content, but rather to create an even texture in order to evaluate typefaces more easily. One may, at a glance, quickly judge the 'colour', or grey value, of a typeface using such a text. Then one may check how easily readabla a text is and how it affects the reader. One may measure how wide or narrow it sets and, upon closer examination, recognize individual letters and their quirks or special features.

As one compares typefaces more and more often, one is eventually

able to identify and name them. Of course, this requires attention to detail and practice. This is dummy text. It is not meant to be read for content, but rather to create an even texture in order to evaluate typefaces more easily. One may, at a glance, quickly judge the 'colour', or grey value, of a typeface using such a text.

Then one may check how easily readable a text is and how it affects the reader. One may measure how wide or narrow it sets and, upon closer examination, recognize individual letters and their quirks or special features. As one compares typefaces more and

more often, one is eventually able to identify and name them. Of course, this requires attention to detail and practice. This is dummy text. It is not meant to be read for content, but rather to create an even texture in order to evaluate typefaces more easily.

One may, at a glance, quickly judge the 'colour', or grey value, of a typeface using such a text. Then one may check how easily readable a text is and how it affects the reader. Of course, this requires attention to detail and practice. This is dummy text. It is not meant to be read for content, but rather to create an even texture

in order to evaluate typefaces more easily. One may, at a glance, quickly judge the 'colour', or grey value, of a typeface using such a text.

Then one may check how easily readable a text is and how it affects the reader. One may measure how wide or narrow it sets and, upon closer examination, recognize individual letters and their quirks or special features. As one compares typefaces more and more often, one is eventually able to identify and name them. Of course, this requires attention to detail and practice. This is dummy text. It is not meant to be

read for content, but rather to create an even texture in order to evaluate typefaces more easily. One may, at a glance, quickly judge the 'colour', or grey value, of a typeface using such a text. Then one may check how easily readable a text is and how it affects the reader.

One may measure how wide or narrow it sets and, upon closer examination, recognize individual letters and their quirks or special features. As one compares typefaces more and more often, one is eventually able to identify and name them. Of course, this requires attention to detail.

3-column grid.

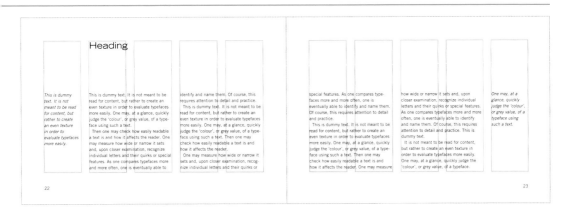

5-column grid. As shown previously, this format enables the designer to accommodate text over all five modules. The designer uses two modules to create a column, leaving a narrower column for secondary information.

6-column grid.
This format gives the designer the option of having text over two module areas, mimicking the 3-column grid, or allowing for module areas each side of the text as indicated.

As the above examples demonstrate, having narrow columns within a grid enables the designer to have more flexibility. Using an odd number of columns can also give the designer a more versatile approach, as secondary information can be displayed adjacent to a main text column and a column can be left empty, creating space.

# Hierarchy of text

Once a grid has been established, the next step is to consider the hierarchy of the information that is to be viewed, such as the title, subtitle, caption, block of text, illustrations and graphic devices. This enables readers to understand how the various components fit together and appreciate the end product.

### Establishing hierarchy

To ensure that users will comprehend the text that is being placed on the grid, designers must first understand it themselves. Having done this, the designer is in a position to decide on an order of importance or hierarchy.

This is one suggested hierarchy. However, it should be noted that hierarchy will vary depending on the nature of the text.

1. Heading
2. Subheading
3. Text
4. Footnotes
5. Headers and / or footers
6. Folios (page numbers)

Once an order has been established within the text, the designer should then begin to emphasize this hierarchy using the following criteria:

1. Choice of typeface (x-height)
2. Paragraph spaces (indented, line spaces etc)
3. Use of type styles (bold, italic, condensed etc)
4. Alignment (ranged left, ranged right, justified, centred)

Keep it simple. The more typefaces, sizes, weights, and graphic elements, such as underlines, rules etc are used, the more difficult a piece will be to design. Don't use more than two (distinctly different) typefaces.

RUNNING HEAD

Heading

This is dummy text. It is not meant to be read for content, but rather to create an even texture in order to evaluate typefaces more easily. One may, at a glance, quickly judge the 'colour', or grey value, of a typeface using such a text. Then one may check how easily readable a text is and how it affects the reader.

One may measure how wide or narrow it sets and, upon closer examination, recognize individual letters and their quirks or special features. As one compares typefaces more and more often, one is eventually able to identify and name them. Of course, this requires attention to detail[1] and practice. This is dummy text. It is not meant to be read for content, but rather to create an even texture in order to evaluate typefaces more easily. One may, at a glance, quickly judge the 'colour', or grey value, of a typeface using such a text. Then one may check how easily readable a text is and how it affects the reader. One may measure how wide or narrow it sets and, upon closer examination, recognize individual letters and their quirks or special features.

Subheading

As one compares typefaces more and more often, one is eventually able to identify and name them. Of course, this requires attention to detail and practice. This is dummy text. It is not meant to be read for content. One may, at a glance, quickly judge the 'colour', or grey value, of a typeface using such a text. Then one may check how easily readable a text is and how it affects the reader. One may measure how wide or narrow it sets and, upon closer examination, recognize individual letters and their quirks or special features. As one compares typefaces more and more often, one is eventually able to identify and name them.

Of course, this requires attention to detail and practice. This is dummy text. It is not meant to be read for content, but rather to create an even texture in order to evaluate typefaces more easily. One may, at a glance, quickly judge the 'colour', or grey value, of a typeface[2] using such a text. Then one may check how easily readable a text is and how it affects.the reader. One may measure how wide or narrow it sets and, upon closer examination, recognize individual letters and their quirks or special features. As one compares typefaces more and more often, one is eventually able to identify and name them.

1 V. Squire, *Getting it Right with Type*, Laurence King Ltd, London 2006, p.445.
2 ibid.

22

This example shows a classic book format. The text is set in a serif typeface and justified. Folios are set at the bottom of the page in line with the outer edge of the column of text.

This example now gives a greater sense of hierarchy. The heading is larger in size, providing a clear focus with which to begin viewing the page. The subheading is in italic and has a line space between the text below, thus reinforcing its place. The text has paragraph spaces, giving the reader smaller, more digestible chunks to absorb. The footnotes are smaller in size, distinguishing them from the main text. The headers are set in a distinctly different typeface. The folios are smaller and more discreet.

Running Head

# HEADING

This is dummy text. It is not meant to be read for content, but rather to create an even texture in order to evaluate typefaces more easily. One may, at a glance, quickly judge the 'colour', or grey value, of a typeface using such a text. Then one may check how easily readable a text is and how it affects the reader.

One may measure how wide or narrow it sets and, upon closer examination, recognize individual letters and their quirks or special features. As one compares typefaces more and more often, one is eventually able to identify and name them. Of course, this requires attention to detail[1] and practice. This is dummy text. It is not meant to be read for content, but rather to create an even texture in order to evaluate typefaces more easily. One may, at a glance, quickly judge the 'colour', or grey value, of a typeface using such a text. Then one may check how easily readable a text is and how it affects the reader. One may measure how wide or narrow it sets and, upon closer examination, recognize individual letters and their quirks or special features.

*Subheading*

As one compares typefaces more and more often, one is eventually able to identify and name them. Of course, this requires attention to detail and practice. This is dummy text. It is not meant to be read for content. One may, at a glance, quickly judge the 'colour', or grey value, of a typeface using such a text. Then one may check how easily readable a text is and how it affects the reader. One may measure how wide or narrow it sets and, upon closer examination, recognize individual letters and their quirks or special features. As one compares typefaces more and more often, one is eventually able to identify and name them.

Of course, this requires attention to detail and practice. This is dummy text. It is not meant to be read for content, but rather to create an even texture in order to evaluate typefaces[2] more easily. One may, at a glance, quickly judge the 'colour', or grey value, of a typeface using such a text. Then one may check how easily readable a text is and how it affects.the reader.

1 V. Squire, *Getting it Right with Type*, Laurence King Ltd, London 2006, p.445.
2 ibid.

22

This is another example of how hierarchy can be achieved, this time using three columns. The subhead is in bold. The text has indented paragraphs. The main text is ranged left. The third column takes the running head and a caption.

# HEADING

This is dummy text. It is not meant to be read for content, but rather to create an even texture in order to evaluate typefaces more easily. One may, at a glance, quickly judge the 'colour', or grey value, of a typeface using such a text.

This is dummy text. It is not meant to be read for content, but rather to create an even texture in order to evaluate typefaces more easily. One may, at a glance, quickly judge the 'colour', or grey value, of a typeface using such a text. Then one may check how easily readable a text is and how it affects the reader.

One may measure how wide or narrow it sets and, upon closer examination, recognize individual letters and their quirks or special features. As one compares typefaces more and more often, one is eventually able to identify and name them. Of course, this requires attention to detail and practice. This is dummy text. It is not meant to be read for content, but rather to create an even texture in order to evaluate typefaces more easily. One may, at a glance, quickly judge the 'colour', or grey value, of a typeface using such a text.

**Subheading**

Then one may check how easily readable a text is and how it affects the reader. One may measure how wide or narrow it sets and, upon closer examination, recognize individual letters and their quirks or special features.

As one compares typefaces more and more often, one is event-ually able to identify and name them. Of course, this requires attention to detail and practice. This is dummy text. It is not meant to be read for content. One may, at a glance, quickly judge the 'colour', or grey value, of a typeface using such a text. Then one may check how easily readable a text is and how it affects the reader. One may measure how wide or narrow it sets and, upon closer examination, recognize individual letters and their quirks or special features. As one compares typefaces more and more often, one is eventually able to identify and name them.

Of course, this requires attention to detail and practice. This is dummy text. It is not meant to be read for content, but rather to create an even texture in order to evaluate typefaces more easily. One may, at a glance, quickly judge the 'colour', or grey value, of a typeface using such a text.

22

Be aware of the binding method. Whether the designed pages will be punched for ring binding, fixed with plastic spines, stapled, glued or book bound, the text column must be correctly positioned. In all cases, the distance from the binding must ensure that reading is not hindered.

The examples on these pages show two pages from a printed report. The text column is pushed well to the right to keep the type away from the left edge which is punched for a particular binding method.

The type is a good, readable sans serif with bold headlines. Paragraphs are separated by full line spaces. Folios are ranged left at the bottom of the text column. Sub-sections are clearly separated with two line spaces above the sub-heading and one below. All the pages, including the title page, begin at the same height and at the left column edge.

Title page.

## Title

This is dummy text.

It is not meant to be read for content, but rather to create an even texture in order to evaluate typefaces more easily.

One may, at a glance, quickly judge the 'colour', or grey value, of a typeface using such a text.

Then one may check how easily readable a text is and how it affects the reader.

22

Of course, this requires attention to detail and practice. This is dummy text. It is not meant to be read for content, but rather to create an even texture in order to evaluate typefaces more easily. One may, at a glance, quickly judge the 'colour', or grey value, of a typeface using such a text.

**Subheading**

This is dummy text. It is not meant to be read for content, but rather to create an even texture in order to evaluate typefaces more easily. One may, at a glance, quickly judge the 'colour', or grey value, of a typeface using such a text. Then one may check how easily readable a text is and how it affects the reader. One may measure how wide or narrow it sets and, upon closer examination, recognize individual letters and their quirks or special features. As one compares typefaces more and more often, one is eventually able to identify and name them. Of course, this requires attention to detail and practice.

This is dummy text. It is not meant to be read for content, but rather to create an even texture in order to evaluate typefaces more easily. One may, at a glance, quickly judge the 'colour', or grey value, of a typeface using such a text.

Then one may check how easily readable a text is and how it affects the reader. One may measure how wide or narrow it sets and, upon closer examination, recognize individual letters and their quirks or special features. As one compares typefaces more and more often, one is event-ually able to identify and name them. Of course, this requires attention to detail and practice. This is dummy text. It is not meant to be read for content. One may, at a glance, quickly judge the 'colour', or grey value, of a typeface using such a text.

Then one may check how easily readable a text is and how it affects the reader. One may measure how wide or narrow it sets and, upon closer examination, recognize individual letters and their quirks or special features.
As one compares typefaces more and more often, one is eventually

23

Text page.

# Hierarchy
# of headings

Many texts are divided into sections such as chapters, which need headings, and divisions of interests within the text, subheadings. Headings and sub-headings are carefully considered in relation to their importance to the reader. Experience shows that four hierarchical levels are a maximum, as more than this can create confusion.

The first-level heading indicates the beginning of a major division in the text.

The second-level heading indicates subsidiary sections of the text at points where the sense calls for a clear break.

The third-level heading functions as a fingerpost to the immediate text topic and need not provide as much of a visual break as the second-level heading.

The fourth-level heading highlights particular points within the text and should not break the visual continuity.

This is dummy text. It is not meant to be read for content, but rather to create an even texture in order to evaluate typefaces more easily. One may, at a glance, quickly judge the 'colour', or grey value, of a typeface using such a text. Then one may check how easily readable a text is and how it affects the reader.

## HEADING 1

As one compares typefaces more and more often, one is eventually able to identify and name them. Of course, this requires attention to detail and practice. This is dummy text. It is not meant to be read for content.

### HEADING 2

Then one may check how easily readable a text is and how it affects the reader. One may measure how wide or narrow it sets and, upon closer examination, recognize individual letters and their quirks or special features.

### HEADING 3
This is dummy text. It is not meant to be read for content. One may, at a glance, quickly judge the 'colour', or grey value, of a typeface using such a text. Then one may check how easily readable a text is and how it affects the reader.

**HEADING 4** One may measure how wide or narrow it sets and, upon closer examination, recognize individual letters and their quirks or special features. As one compares type-faces more and more often, one is eventually able to identify and name them.

Example 1.

This example shows a heading hierarchy with four levels. The hierarchy must be understandable and show the headings' state of importance within the text even when they don't all appear on the same page. Note the use of spacing between the headings and the text.

The first-level heading is indicated through an increase in type size.

The second-level heading is set in bold.

Third-level heading is in italic.

The fourth-level heading is in small caps.

This is dummy text. It is not meant to be read for content, but rather to create an even texture in order to evaluate typefaces more easily. One may, at a glance, quickly judge the 'colour', or grey value, of a typeface using such a text. Then one may check how easily readable a text is and how it affects the reader.

# Heading 1

As one compares typefaces more and more often, one is eventually able to identify and name them. Of course, this requires attention to detail and practice. This is dummy text. It is not meant to be read for content.

**Heading 2**

Then one may check how easily readable a text is and how it affects the reader. One may measure how wide or narrow it sets and, upon closer examination, recognize individual letters and their quirks or special features.

*Heading 3*
This is dummy text. It is not meant to be read for content. One may, at a glance, quickly judge the 'colour', or grey value, of a typeface using such a text. Then one may check how easily readable a text is and how it affects the reader.

HEADING 4 One may measure how wide or narrow it sets and, upon closer examination, recognize individual letters and their quirks or special features. As one compares typefaces more and more often, one is eventually able to identify and name them.

Example 2.

# Page layout
# guidelines

Note:
• Design magazines or books in spreads rather than single pages.
• Do not design the most difficult spreads first, but leave these until the standard spreads have been designed so that the majority of problems will have been addressed.

Once a hierarchy of text has been established, the next stage is to produce a page layout. This section outlines some guidelines to assist the designer in producing such a set of layouts.

In traditional page layout, margins are as follows: the inner margin ('gutter' or 'back') is smaller than the head; the head is smaller than the 'fore-edge', which is in turn smaller than the 'tail', or foot margin.

Folios should be placed outside the type area or at the bottom of the page at least two line spaces below the last line.

• Lines of text should, as far as possible, hold register; that is, should appear to 'back each other up' when the page is held up to the light.
• Ensure that the use of 'white' space is appropriate and does not interrupt the reader's flow.

• If designing a number of spreads, check the visual flow and pace. This ensures that the reader is not disrupted and also that the visual pace is not monotonous but displays variety.

Titles should generally be set ranged left with line breaks according to sense. Even almost full lines should not be justified to the full measure.

Incorrect.

Correct.

A title that naturally falls near the foot of a page should ideally be followed by several lines of the succeeding paragraph. If this is not possible, the title should move to the top of the next page.

Incorrect.

Correct.

# Text and image relationships

When designing with text and images it is essential to ensure that the arrangement of the images is based on their form and content, and not on formal typographic guidelines. The proportions of a layout should be determined by the format and proportions of the images, not the other way around.

Images beside and above each other should not be observed in isolation, but should rather be viewed as being influenced by their neighbours. Designers should not leave this image-to-image relation-ship to chance. They must see to it that the images enhance, rather than interfere with each other. This depends on various components:

• the proportions of the image area;

• their weight (dark or light);

• their formal and contextual activity;

• the possibility of image continuation.

The following examples show a range of problems with image positioning that result from their particular contexts.

The one-way sign on the left points away into the distance; the one on the right threatens catastrophe!

The sign on the left visually allows the three alternative roads to be used. Exactly the same sign on the right prevents the A110 to Enfield from being undertaken. The position alone can change the message of an image.

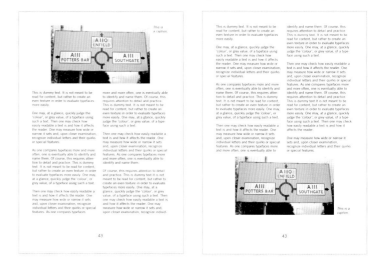

'Caution: blind hill'. One cannot so easily evade this message when it comes directly out of the middle of the page. Banned to the bottom, as shown on the right, the sign takes on the quality of an insignificant comment.

When the two images correspond contextually and formally, the design works.

When the images have little
commonality, formally or contextually,
it can be disagreeable.

This is dummy text. It is not meant to be read for content, but rather to create an even texture in order to evaluate typefaces more easily. One may, at a glance, quickly judge the 'colour', or grey value, of a typeface using such a text. Then one may check how easily readable a text is and how it affects the reader. One may measure how wide or narrow in sets and, upon closer examination, recognize individual letters and their quirks or special features. As one compares typefaces more and more often, one is eventually able to identify and name them. Of course, this requires attention to detail and practice. This is dummy text. It is not meant to be read for content, but rather to create an even texture in order to evaluate typefaces more easily. One may, at a glance, quickly judge the 'colour', or grey value, of a typeface using such a text.

Then one may check how easily readable a text is and how it affects the reader. One may measure how wide or narrow it sets and, upon closer examination, recognize individual letters and their quirks or special features. As one compares typefaces more and more often, one is eventually able to identify and name them. Of course, this requires attention to detail and practice. This is dummy text. It is not meant to be read for content, but rather to create an even texture in order to evaluate typefaces more easily. One may, at a glance, quickly judge the 'colour', or grey value, of a typeface using such a text. Then one may check how easily readable a text is and how it affects the reader.

*This is a caption. It is not meant to be read for content.*

read for content, but rather to create an even texture in order to evaluate typefaces more easily. One may, at a glance, quickly judge the 'colour', or grey value, of a typeface using such a text.

One may measure how wide or narrow it sets and, upon closer examination, recognize individual letters and their quirks or special features. As one compares typefaces more and more often.

43

These two design solutions reduce the discrepancy of the images by
separating them on the page.

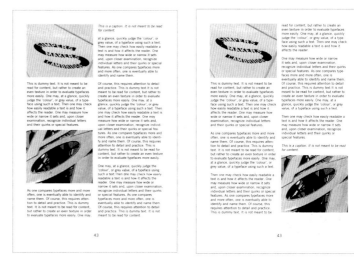

This is dummy text. It is not meant to be read for content, but rather to create an even texture in order to evaluate typefaces more easily. One may, at a glance, quickly judge the 'colour', or grey value, of a typeface using such a text. Then one may check how easily readable a text is and how it affects the reader. One may measure how wide or narrow it sets and, upon closer examination, recognize individual letters and their quirks or special features.

As one compares typefaces more and more often, one is eventually able to identify and name them. Of course, this requires attention to detail and practice. This is dummy text. It is not meant to be read for content, but rather to create an even texture in order to evaluate typefaces more easily. One may.

*This is a caption. It is not meant to be read for content.*

at a glance, quickly judge the 'colour', or grey value, of a typeface using such a text. Then one may check how easily readable a text is and how it affects the reader. One may measure how wide or narrow it sets and, upon closer examination, recognize individual letters and their quirks or special features. As one compares typefaces more and more often, one is eventually able to identify and name them.

Of course, this requires attention to detail and practice. This is dummy text. It is not meant to be read for content, but rather to create an even texture in order to evaluate typefaces more easily. One may, at a glance, quickly judge the 'colour', or grey value, of a typeface using such a text. Then one may check how easily readable a text is and how it affects the reader. One may measure how wide or narrow it sets and, upon closer examination, recognize individual letters and their quirks or special features. As one compares typefaces more and more often, one is eventually able to identify and name them. Of course, this requires attention to detail and practice. This is dummy text. It is not meant to be read for content, but rather to create an even texture in order to evaluate typefaces more easily.

One may, at a glance, quickly judge the 'colour', or grey value, of a typeface using such a text. Then one may check how easily readable a text is and how it affects the reader. One may measure how wide or narrow it sets and, upon closer examination, recognize individual letters and their quirks or special features. As one compares typefaces more and more often, one is eventually able to identify and name them. Of course, this requires attention to detail and practice. This is dummy text. It is not meant to be read for content

43

read for content, but rather to create an even texture in order to evaluate typefaces more easily. One may, at a glance, quickly judge the 'colour', or grey value, of a typeface using such a text. Then one may check how easily readable a text is and how it affects the reader.

One may measure how wide or narrow it sets and, upon closer examination, recognize individual letters and their quirks or special features. As one compares typefaces more and more often, one is eventually able to identify and name them. Of course, this requires attention to detail and practice. This is dummy text. It is not meant to be read for content, but rather to create an even texture in order to evaluate typefaces more easily. One may, at a glance, quickly judge the 'colour', or grey value, of a typeface using such a text.

Then one may check how easily readable a text is and how it affects the reader. One may measure how wide or narrow it sets and, upon closer examination, recognize individual letters and their quirks or special features.

*This is a caption. It is not meant to be read for content.*

43

Sometimes images can complement each other but fit too well together and seem too similar, implying a connection that may not exist.
(In this example both signs are from the same area, Lincolnshire in the UK; however, they indicate different place names.)

Two design solutions highlight the difference by changing the shape of one of the picture boxes and then moving the position of one of the images.

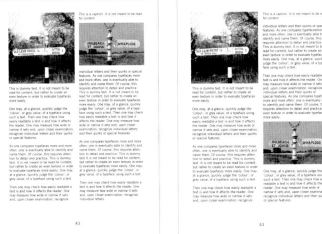

# Footnotes
# and bibliographies

Wanting to look something up and not being able to find it – quite often this can be due to poor typography. This is as valid for large dictionaries as for the details of footnotes, indexes and tables of contents.

The earlier part of this chapter focused on the grid, text in columns, headings and text–image relationships. This section gives an overview of different reference elements within book design such as footnotes, bibliographies, tables of contents and indexes.

## Footnotes

Reference numbers within texts are an indication to readers that a footnote is available, which they may follow up or ignore. These figures are set in a small size and raised up from the baseline (superscript). They should also be positioned outside punctuation, such as a full point. The reader who takes up the offer and searches for the footnote must of course be able to find it. Where a chapter may have very few footnotes (not more than two or three on any one page) there is the option of using reference marks rather than numbers, such as †, ‡ etc (see Appendix 1). The typesize of footnotes must be noticeably smaller than the basic text size. Ranged-left setting is recommended in texts that are heavily structured by names and dates.

This is dummy text. It is not meant to be read for content, but rather to create an even texture in order to evaluate typefaces more easily. One may, at a glance, quickly judge the 'colour', or grey value, of a typeface[1] using such a text. Then one may check how easily readable a text is and how it affects the reader. One may measure how wide or narrow it sets and, upon closer examination, recognize individual letters and their quirks or special features.[2] As one compares typefaces more and more often, one is eventually able to identify and name them. Of course, this requires attention to detail and practice.

1. The typesize of footnotes must be noticeably smaller than the basic text size.
2. The footnote indicator should be positioned outside punctuation.

Footnotes appear on the same page as their corresponding reference figure or mark (although sometimes all the notes are gathered at the back of a book as endnotes). Where the footnote continues over a page, at least three lines of text should be present. The reference figure or mark should ideally be placed in the last line of text on the page. Another method used when a footnote runs over a page is the practice of placing a short, ranged-left rule above the footnote text, indicating a run over.

## Bibliographies

Bibliographies are frequently heavily structured and are therefore preferably set ranged left avoiding hyphenation. This allows the viewer to follow the information easily, avoiding the separation of parts of dates, names and other data.

Depending on complexity, a bibliography may be set throughout in one typeface or may be differentiated through bold, italic and normal, using a variety of type styles. The use of small capitals – in principle appropriate – demands a more refined procedure.

Author names are bold and indented, with book titles in italic.

**Phil Baines and Andrew Haslam,** *Type & Typography*, London, Laurence King Publishing, 2002
**Lewis Blackwell,** *Twentieth-Century Type* (revised edn), London, Laurence King Publishing, 2004
**Christopher Perfect and Gordon Rookledge,** *Rookledge's Classic International Typefinder*, London, Laurence King Publishing, 2004
**John Kane,** *A Type Primer*, London, Laurence King Publishing, 2002

All set in one typeface and style; authors' names are set on hanging indents.

Phil Baines and Andrew Haslam, Type & Typography, London,
    Laurence King Publishing, 2002
Lewis Blackwell, Twentieth-Century Type (revised edn), London,
    Laurence King Publishing, 2004
Christopher Perfect and Gordon Rookledge, Rookledge's Classic
International Typefinder, London, Laurence King Publishing, 2004
John Kane, A Type Primer, London, Laurence King Publishing, 2002

All set in one typeface, but with the book title in italic.

Phil Baines and Andrew Haslam, *Type & Typography*, London,
    Laurence King Publishing, 2002
Lewis Blackwell, *Twentieth-Century Type* (revised edn), London,
    Laurence King Publishing, 2004
Christopher Perfect and Gordon Rookledge, *Rookledge's Classic
    International Typefinder*, London, Laurence King Publishing, 2004
John Kane, *A Type Primer*, London, Laurence King Publishing, 2002

Entries are separated by half-line spaces. Indents are therefore superfluous.

Phil Baines and Andrew Haslam, *Type & Typography*, London,
Laurence King Publishing, 2002

Lewis Blackwell, *Twentieth-Century Type* (revised edn), London,
Laurence King Publishing, 2004

Christopher Perfect and Gordon Rookledge, *Rookledge's Classic
International Typefinder*, London, Laurence King Publishing, 2004

John Kane, *A Type Primer*, London, Laurence King Publishing, 2002

# Contents

Tables of contents are invariably difficult to design. Ensuring that the reader can find a particular item when looking something up is never a straightforward task. The following are a few of the most reasonably safe tips for the beginner when designing all kinds of tables of contents:

• Lines are to be set ranged left and broken according to sense. Even almost full lines are not to be justified to the full measure.

• Title hierarchy should be comprehensible at a glance, not only through the arrangement, but also through the typography.

• Title hierarchy in the table of contents need not precisely 'mirror' the title style within the text; it should, however, correspond to the character of the internal typography.

• Page numbers within a table of contents should be treated with consistency and should not change according to the style of the text that the page number corresponds to.

• Run-on lines are set using the same line spacing.

• Lines in the table of contents should hold register or, if applicable, half-line register (shifted vertically by half a line). Pages of the table of contents need not run to the same depth.

The following examples show possible levels of hierarchy within a table of contents using a variety of type styles. All three examples are set in the same typesize but show levels of hierarchy through the use of indents, type style and line spacing.

The four levels of hierarchy are:
bold without indent;
normal without indent;
normal with indent;
italic with indent.

Ordinal numbers are set to a common left axis and are not emphasized through bold or italic. Subheading lines also have a common left axis. There is a half-line space above and below primary heads. Otherwise this is set as the first example.

Emphases of ordinal numbers and letters correspond to their lines. They are arranged on a common left axis, the same as the lines themselves.

The four levels of hierarchy:
bold, with half-line space above and below;
bold, with no line space;
normal;
italic, ordinal numbers indented.

The following examples show a variety of ways in which reference numbers can be set within tables of contents.

It is customary in tables of contents to place the reference numbers at the far right of the column. One then needs the help of a ruler. With short lines and a wide column, it's easy to lose the continuity and make a mistake in finding the page number you're looking for.

Old-fashioned 'leader dots' serve to guide the eye across the page. There should be roughly one word space between the dots and they should sit directly above and below each other; that is, not staggered. The space before and after dot rows should be larger than a normal word space.

If page numbers are positioned directly after table entries, it is then clear, without additional help, what belongs together. If numbers (for example, dates) appear at the end of entries, one must use an en dash, with a word space before and after, to separate entries from their page numbers.

A two-column table of contents, set justified and without leader dots, can lead to the numbers from one column appearing to belong to the wrong column. This arrangement is best avoided.

A two-column table of contents should always be set with page numbers directly following their entries.

# Indexes

Indexes are, as a rule, set in two or three columns which do not need to be the same in depth. Index type can be quite small as one tends not to read too much of it at once.

Indexes should always be set ranged left; even almost-full lines are not to be justified to the full column measure. Run-on lines should be indented.

abbreviations 17
accents 8
acronyms 49, 150
Akzidenz Grotesk 36, 38, 91
alphabets 60, 75, 79, 95, 96, 103,
    105, 130
ampersand 5, 19, 21, 37, 47, 53, 59
    65, 67, 69-71, 77, 115, 118, 121,

125, 132, 137, 155, 160
apex 59
apostrophes 39-44, 62, 65
Arial 113
artwork 50, 5-55, 101, 109, 113,
    120, 125-7
ascenders 116
Ashley Script 143-5, 156, 160-1, 169

Here is an example for triple differentiation of reference numbers using Roman, bold and italic type styles. Italic indicates a picture reference and bold indicates a table or diagram. The designer needs to make this distinction clear to the reader at the start of the index.

A functional index may be created using quite simple typography, but multiple typographic differentiations may also be quite practical.

**abbreviations** 17
**accents** 8
**acronyms** 49, *150*
**Akzidenz Grotesk** 36, 38, 91
**alphabets** 60, 75, **79**, **95**, 96, *103*
    105, 130
**ampersand** 5, 19, 21, **37**, *47*, 53, 59,
    65, 67, **69**, **71**, 77, 115, 118, 121,

125, **132**, *137*, 155, 160
**apex** 59
**apostrophes** 39-44, **62**, 65
**Arial** 113
**artwork** 50, 52-5, *101*, 109, 113,
    **120**, 125-7
**ascenders** 116
**Ashley Script** 143-5, **156**, 160-1, 169

# Tabular and tabled information

Examples of table design are found all around us in bus or train timetables, weather charts, breakdowns of statistics and finances. This information usually needs to be read horizontally as well as vertically and often simultaneously, but the design of the table must be dependent on the content of the material to be read.

It is essential to choose a clear and readable typeface when designing tables, and it does not necessarily need to follow that of the main text. If numerals are to be used, and are to be read continuously, it may be preferable to use lining numerals, particularly if they are set in a small size. Therefore, with both text and numerals, comprehension and clarity should be achieved through the simplest possible means.

Note that, as usual, multiple-line entries in headings, as well as in 'boxes', should be broken by sense.

| Monday to Friday (except public holidays) LONGMONT–ROZELLE via VICTORIA | | | | | | | |
|---|---|---|---|---|---|---|---|
| Service No. | 310 | 310 | 310 | 310 | 310 | 310 | 310 |
| LONGMONT Bus Station | ---- | 1020 | 1120 | 1220 | 1320 | 1420 | 1520 |
| Walton Way | ---- | ---- | 1127 | 1227 | ---- | 1427 | 1527 |
| Boulder Cross | 0900 | ---- | 1130 | 1230 | ---- | 1430 | 1530 |
| Victoria | 0910 | ---- | 1140 | 1240 | ---- | 1440 | 1540 |
| District Hospital | ---- | 1025 | ---- | ---- | 1325 | ---- | ---- |
| General Stores | ---- | 1031 | ---- | ---- | 1331 | ---- | ---- |
| Court Turn | ---- | 1040 | ---- | ---- | 1340 | ---- | ---- |
| Ford Shelter | ---- | 1043 | ---- | ---- | 1343 | ---- | ---- |
| Easterclose | ---- | ---- | ---- | ---- | 1346 | ---- | ---- |
| Applecross Gate | 0920 | 1050 | 1150 | 1250 | 1355 | 1450 | 1550 |
| Greenwood | 0925 | 1055 | 1155 | 1255 | 1400 | 1455 | 1555 |
| Mountain Hilltop | 0937 | 1107 | 1207 | 1307 | 1412 | 1507 | 1607 |
| ROZELLE | 0943 | 1113 | 1213 | 1313 | 1418 | 1513 | 1613 |

Notes: *School days only*

An unclear table with information centred in the boxes and a poor choice of typeface, size and leading.

Monday to Friday (except public holidays)
LONGMONT–ROZELLE via VICTORIA

| Service No. | 310 | 310 | 310 | 310 | 310 | 310 | 310 |
|---|---|---|---|---|---|---|---|
| LONGMONT Bus Station | ---- | 1020 | 1120 | 1220 | 1320 | 1420 | 1520 |
| Walton Way | ---- | ---- | 1127 | 1227 | ---- | 1427 | 1527 |
| Boulder Cross | 0900 | ---- | 1130 | 1230 | ---- | 1430 | 1530 |
| Victoria | 0910 | ---- | 1140 | 1240 | ---- | 1440 | 1540 |
| District Hospital | ---- | 1025 | ---- | ---- | 1325 | ---- | ---- |
| General Stores | ---- | 1031 | ---- | ---- | 1331 | ---- | ---- |
| Court Turn | ---- | 1040 | ---- | ---- | 1340 | ---- | ---- |
| Ford Shelter | ---- | 1043 | ---- | ---- | 1343 | ---- | ---- |
| Easterclose | ---- | ---- | ---- | ---- | 1346 | ---- | ---- |
| Applecross Gate | 0920 | 1050 | 1150 | 1250 | 1355 | 1450 | 1550 |
| Greenwood | 0925 | 1055 | 1155 | 1255 | 1400 | 1455 | 1555 |
| Mountain Hilltop | 0937 | 1107 | 1207 | 1307 | 1412 | 1507 | 1607 |
| ROZELLE | 0943 | 1113 | 1213 | 1313 | 1418 | 1513 | 1613 |

Notes: *School days only*

The same table is made more readable by the choice of typeface (larger x-height and open counters). Information is ranged left, the rules have been removed and replaced by line spaces.

**Monday to Friday (except public holidays)**

LONGMONT–ROZELLE via VICTORIA

| Service No. | 310 | 310 | 310 | 310 | 310 | 310 | 310 |
|---|---|---|---|---|---|---|---|
| LONGMONT Bus Station | ---- | **1020** | **1120** | 1220 | 1320 | *1420* | *1520* |
| Walton Way | ---- | ---- | **1127** | 1227 | ---- | *1427* | *1527* |
| Boulder Cross | **0900** | ---- | **1130** | 1230 | ---- | *1430* | *1530* |
| Victoria | **0910** | ---- | **1140** | 1240 | ---- | *1440* | *1540* |
| District Hospital | ---- | **1025** | ---- | ---- | 1325 | ---- | ---- |
| General Stores | ---- | **1031** | ---- | ---- | 1331 | ---- | ---- |
| Court Turn | ---- | **1040** | ---- | ---- | 1340 | ---- | ---- |
| Ford Shelter | ---- | **1043** | ---- | ---- | 1343 | ---- | ---- |
| Easterclose | ---- | ---- | ---- | ---- | 1346 | ---- | ---- |
| Applecross Gate | **0920** | **1050** | **1150** | 1250 | 1355 | *1450* | *1550* |
| Greenwood | **0925** | **1055** | **1155** | 1255 | 1400 | *1455* | *1555* |
| Mountain Hilltop | **0937** | **1107** | 1207 | 1307 | 1412 | *1507* | *1607* |
| ROZELLE | **0943** | **1113** | 1213 | 1313 | 1418 | *1513* | *1613* |

Notes: *School days only*

The same table again, this time placing emphasis on days of the week, service number and distinguishing between the a.m. and p.m. times.

**Monday to Friday (except public holidays)**

LONGMONT–ROZELLE via VICTORIA

| Service No. | 310 | 310 | 310 | 310 | 310 | 310 | 310 |
|---|---|---|---|---|---|---|---|
| LONGMONT Bus Station | ---- | 1020 | 1120 | 1220 | 1320 | 1420 | 1520 |
| Walton Way | ---- | ---- | 1127 | 1227 | ---- | 1427 | 1527 |
| Boulder Cross | 0900 | ---- | 1130 | 1230 | ---- | 1430 | 1530 |
| Victoria | 0910 | ---- | 1140 | 1240 | ---- | 1440 | 1540 |
| District Hospital | ---- | 1025 | ---- | ---- | 1325 | ---- | ---- |
| General Stores | ---- | 1031 | ---- | ---- | 1331 | ---- | ---- |
| Court Turn | ---- | 1040 | ---- | ---- | 1340 | ---- | ---- |
| Ford Shelter | ---- | 1043 | ---- | ---- | 1343 | ---- | ---- |
| Easterclose | ---- | ---- | ---- | ---- | 1346 | ---- | ---- |
| Applecross Gate | 0920 | 1050 | 1150 | 1250 | 1355 | 1450 | 1550 |
| Greenwood | 0925 | 1055 | 1155 | 1255 | 1400 | 1455 | 1555 |
| Mountain Hilltop | 0937 | 1107 | 1207 | 1307 | 1412 | 1507 | 1607 |
| ROZELLE | 0943 | 1113 | 1213 | 1313 | 1418 | 1513 | 1613 |

Notes: *School days only* ▦

This time the hierarchy has been reinforced by the use of rules and information within screened boxes.

# 4

# Typography

## Print and screen

Covering:
Print and screen technical terminology
Type and paper
Type legibility
Type reproduction
Printing
Binding
Type on screen

# Typography:
# print and screen

Many designers generate accomplished layouts with well-considered use of typography, but do not pay enough attention to how the design is to be produced and what it is being produced for. It is essential to establish a rationale for the reproduction of type on a chosen paper stock using a particular print process, or on a computer screen as static information or moving typography, because these factors can make or break a design.

The previous chapters introduced you to the basics of designing with typography, enabling you to explore the subject and work with it in a professional manner within a variety of contexts. This chapter examines the typographic considerations that have to be made when designing work to be printed or to be viewed on screen. It will give you an understanding of print (printing processes, ink, papers and binding) as well as the screen-based use of typography.

When designing for print, consideration should be given to:
• paper stock
• paper and typographic legibility / readability
• print processes and reproduction
• typography and binding

When designing for screen, consideration should be given to:
• screen-based typographic legibility / readability
• colour of type / choice of background
• static or animated type
• screen resolution

# Print and screen: technical terminology

The following are technical terms which are used within this chapter. It is important to familiarize yourself with them in order to fully understand and have a thorough awareness of the subject.

## Paper stock

antique wove
Paper with a slightly rough surface.

board
The industrial term for card.

calendering
A process used to smooth paper during manufacturing, without adding a clay coating.

card
A thick stiff paper.

gloss-coated art paper
Paper coated with a clay substance during manufacture and having a smooth, shiny surface.

grain
The direction in which paper fibres lie.

matte-coated
Paper coated with a smooth but non-shiny clay surface.

ream
500 sheets of paper. See also Appendix 2, p.170, for paper sizes.

## Printing

bleed
The area of an image extending beyond the trim marks of a page.

CMYK
Cyan, magenta, yellow and black – the four process colours used in offset printing.

digital proofing
Producing page proofs directly from stored digital files without using film or plates.

dtp 'desktop publishing'
The design and production of print through the use of a computer.

dummy
A mock-up of the product produced prior to publication. This is to demonstrate the size, shape and features, and acts as a guide for production.

duotone
A two-colour printing process usually used for photographs or illustrations.

EPS
(Encapsulated PostScript file). A standard format capable of holding both vector and bitmap information.

halftone
A method of reproducing photographs and illustrations where grey tones are represented by varying sizes of fine black dots.

laser printer
A xerographic printing device using a laser to create letterforms and images on paper.

letterpress
Printing process using raised metal or wooden letterforms which are inked for transfer to paper.

offset printing
Printing process in which ink is transferred from a stone or plate to a rubber surface which is then transferred to paper.

pantone
An international colour-matching system for printing.

photosetting
A typesetting technology using light projected through film discs or strips.

process colours
Cyan, magenta, yellow, black – four process-colour inks used in printing.

proof
A visual interpretation of a document to be printed.

registration marks
Marks that are used to check that colours line up.

rotogravure
A printing method, ideally suited to photographic images, characterized by soft, smooth tones.

screen
A process using a piece of glass or plastic to create a halftone from a continuous tone.

screenprinting
Printing process in which ink is forced through a fine fabric (originally silk) onto a surface such as paper.

TIFF
(Tagged Image File Format). Used for storing bitmapped or scanned images.

tint
A tonal area of a colour.

## Print effects

### die-cutting
Process using sharp rules to cut shapes from printed sheets.

### die-stamping / blocking
Process using an engraved, depressed image to produce an embossed, relief effect.

### embossing
A process which enables typography to stand in relief on the surface of the paper.

### foil-stamping / blocking
Use of a relief block to transfer metallized type by the use of controlled pressure.

### varnish / lamination
A coating that is applied to a printed document and used for protection or appearance.

## Binding

### gutter
The combined margin of a book on each side of the spine.

### imposition
The layout of pages on a printing plate so that when a publication is printed and bound they come out in the correct order.

### perfect binding
A binding method used for magazines and paperback books where cut sheets are glued together at the back and held to a cover.

### quire
A collection of leaves, one within another, in a book.

### scoring
A manufacturing process whereby a metal rule is pressed into the paper or card to enable cleaner folding.

### section
A large sheet of paper on which multiple pages are printed in preparation for folding and cutting.

### signature
A figure or mark placed on a section and used as a guide for binding.

### spine
The part of the book cover that encloses and protects the stitching.

### stitching
A method used to bind pages of a book, pamphlet etc with wire stapes or thread.

## Screen / digital

### bitmaps
1. An image composed of pixels.
2. The representation of a font on screen.

### CD-ROM.
Compact Disc, Read-Only Memory.

### colour (typography)
The tone of a typeface or block of text on a computer screen.

### digitalization
Converting information into digital form, which is stored and represented through binary data.

### GIF
(Graphics Interchange Format). A method of storing bitmap images for use on the Internet in a compressed format.

### HTML
(HyperText Mark-up Language). Used for creating web pages.

### jaggies
Rough edges of curved or sloped forms as represented on computer screens.

### JPEG
(Joint Photographic Experts Group). A lossy compression format for continuous-tone image files.

### PDA
(Personal Digital Assistant). A hand-held computer that serves as an organizer for personal information.

### pixel (picture element)
Dots on screen used to render an image.

### vectors
Objects defined by mathematical points on a computer screen.

### Wysiwyg
(what you see is what you get). What you see on a screen is what you will get as a printed output (although only as accurate as the screen can render).

# Paper and reading

The paper that is chosen for a job can change the whole appearance of the typography. A small block of text on shiny paper being read in the sun can be tiring for the reader, whilst a book with the grain set in the wrong direction can cause noise and rustling when turning the page. The designer should also consider how the paper will bend, fold and feel.

Printing paper is complicated material. There are so many varieties – thick or thin, smooth or rough, matt or coated – which can be printed on one or both sides. Paper also comes in a range of weights, thicknesses and sizes.

## An exploration of paper
A few characteristic features:
- It can be wood-free, i.e. made of cellulose.
- It can be woody, i.e. with an amount of wood fibre.
- It can be more or less opaque or transparent.
- It can be tinted in various ways.
- It comes in various weights, defined as grams per square metre in the UK and pounds in the US. The weight does not provide an indication of the paper thickness. Heavier weights are usually classified as card.
- It can have different 'volumes', i.e. contain varying amounts of air.
- It is distributed in reams or reels.

## Natural papers
Natural papers are made only of a mix of fibres, with some additives. They can have:
- a raw surface;
- a somewhat smoother surface (machine-finish);
- a very smooth (satin) finish.

## Coated papers
Coated papers have their surfaces sealed with a thin coating of clay material. There are:
- calendered offset papers;
- art papers.

Paper is *hydroscopic*; that is, it takes up moisture from, and gives up moisture to, the air. This means that it expands and shrinks. This matters little for single sheets, but plays a role where pamphlets or books are concerned. All the attributes of paper have an effect on the character of a printed piece, though several of these characteristics have particular importance for design.

## Grain direction
Paper has a grain direction. During production, paper pulp is poured onto a huge, rapidly moving sieve. The fibres are aligned by this process, giving the grain direction. Correct grain direction is when the paper fibres are aligned parallel with the spine of the book. Incorrect grain direction is when the paper fibres run perpendicular to the spine of the book.

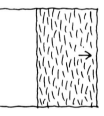 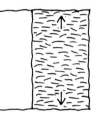

In the above illustration, the lines refer to the direction of the paper fibres, the arrows to the direction in which the fibres stretch. When the grain direction is correct, the paper is free to stretch in the direction of the arrows. When it is wrong, the paper wants to stretch vertically but is unable because it's glued to the spine. Paper will not easily bend or fold against the grain.

## Paper thickness / weight
When choosing paper the thickness must be taken into account as it will determine the overall thickness of the item to be produced. If this is a book or document it will affect the width of the spine. When designing such an item it is desirable to produce a 'dummy' version to enable the shape, size, weight and feel to be fully considered.

## Paper surface, colour and reading

Knowledge of the effects of the surface and colour of paper will assist with the choice of typeface. Brochures for cars, jewellery or investments require brilliance. Specialist medicine or art books require colour fidelity; white, coated paper, if possible with a glossy finish, is appropriate here.

Images and type can spread on porous paper while a very smooth paper finish can cause reflection which can make the type start to swim before the eye. When using particularly white paper with black text, producing a strong contrast, it can leave the reader feeling a little dazzled.

## Type and paper

The contrast between bright-white paper (which is actually tinted with a bit of blue) and deep-black type can be overwhelming. If a bright-white paper is needed for clear reproduction of illustrations, then don't use type with strong thick–thin contrast or type which is too light.

When type is printed in a sepia tone in order to alleviate the dazzling effect of too-high contrast, this can lead to a soft, washed-out result which also affects legibility. Regardless of paper colour, very glossy coated papers lean toward a 'glaring' effect which can be detrimental to easy reading.

Type printed on recycled paper is as a rule easy to read. It should not, however, be too thin or too lightly printed.

With tinted or brightly coloured papers, one should do a test print to see which typefaces are up to the challenge.

Legibility can also depend to a large extent on how transparent the paper is. If paper has a low opacity, you can see what's on the previous, or next, page. This can disrupt easy reading. In this case, the typography must be appropriately arranged so that lines correspond exactly on the front and back of the sheet; that is, they are kept 'in register'. This of course also depends on accurate printing.

To achieve effective results with paper it is essential to plan a job and test effects of typography on the paper prior to sending the job to print. It is vital to encourage a good working relationship with printers as they will be able to assist further with paper choice. It is also possible to obtain samples of paper and board direct from paper merchants.

The effects of different combinations of type, paper finish and paper colour are demonstrated on the following pages.

# 1

# Eight faces
# on four papers

Like most sans-serif faces, Frutiger suits white and gloss-coated papers. This typeface also works well with practically all other surfaces.

This is dummy text. It is not meant to be read for content, but rather to create an even texture in order to evaluate typefaces more easily. One may, at a glance, quickly judge the 'colour', or grey value, of a typeface using such a text. Then one may check how easily readable a text is and how it affects the reader. One may measure how wide or narrow it sets and, upon closer examination, recognize individual letters and their quirks or special features. As one compares typefaces more and more often, one is eventually able to identify and name them.

Bolder sans-serif typefaces, like Helvetica Semibold, for example, sit well on off-white papers. On bright-white papers they tend to sparkle. Counters (the inner shapes of letterforms) become active. This can have an aesthetic charm but doesn't exactly aid legibility.

**This is dummy text. It is not meant to be read for content, but rather to create an even texture in order to evaluate typefaces more easily. One may, at a glance, quickly judge the 'colour', or grey value, of a typeface using such a text. Then one may check how easily readable a text is and how it affects the reader. One may measure how wide or narrow it sets and, upon closer examination, recognize individual letters and their quirks or special features. As one compares typefaces more and more often, one is eventually able to identify and name them.**

The example of News Gothic shows that even a good, readable sans-serif face can get into difficulties if it's too light. The white paper floods the delicate body of the type.

This is dummy text. It is not meant to be read for content, but rather to create an even texture in order to evaluate typefaces more easily. One may, at a glance, quickly judge the 'colour', or grey value, of a typeface using such a text. Then one may check how easily readable a text is and how it affects the reader. One may measure how wide or narrow it sets and, upon closer examination, recognize individual letters and their quirks or special features. As one compares typefaces more and more often, one is eventually able to identify and name them. Of course, this requires attention to detail and practice.

Typefaces with slab serifs, such as Rockwell, can as a rule take quite a lot of wear and tear, even as far as paper is concerned. But also here one must be careful with very light weights (danger of 'flooding') or very heavy weights (danger of 'sparkling').

This is dummy text. It is not meant to be read for content, but rather to create an even texture in order to evaluate typefaces more easily. One may, at a glance, quickly judge the 'colour', or grey value, of a typeface using such a text. Then one may check how easily readable a text is and how it affects the reader. One may measure how wide or narrow it sets and, upon closer examination, recognize individual letters and their quirks or special features. As one compares typefaces more and more often, one is eventually able to identify and name them.

# 2

# Eight faces
# on four papers

When the modern typeface Bodoni is printed on bright-white paper, it's hard to recognize what an attractive typeface it really is. It flickers before the eyes because the strong thick–thin contrast is excessively increased. The white of the paper bleaches out the fine strokes.

This is dummy text. It is not meant to be read for content, but rather to create an even texture in order to evaluate typefaces more easily. One may, at a glance, quickly judge the 'colour', or grey value, of a typeface using such a text. Then one may check how easily readable a text is and how it affects the reader. One may measure how wide or narrow it sets and, upon closer examination, recognize individual letters and their quirks or special features. As one compares typefaces more and more often, one is eventually able to identify and name them.

White paper doesn't hurt the old face typeface Garamond quite as much since the stroke-weight contrast is less. Nonetheless it still feels a bit out of place.

This is dummy text. It is not meant to be read for content, but rather to create an even texture in order to evaluate typefaces more easily. One may, at a glance, quickly judge the 'colour', or grey value, of a typeface using such a text. Then one may check how easily readable a text is and how it affects the reader. One may measure how wide or narrow it sets and, upon closer examination, recognize individual letters and their quirks or special features. As one compares typefaces more and more often, one is eventually able to identify and name them.

The transitional typeface Times Roman is not as insensitive as its reputation would have us believe. On bright-white paper it tends to appear uneven or blotchy. It was, after all, originally designed to be used on newsprint.

This is dummy text. It is not meant to be read for content, but rather to create an even texture in order to evaluate typefaces more easily. One may, at a glance, quickly judge the 'colour', or grey value, of a typeface using such a text. Then one may check how easily readable a text is and how it affects the reader. One may measure how wide or narrow it sets and, upon closer examination, recognize individual letters and their quirks or special features. As one compares typefaces more and more often, one is eventually able to identify and name them.

The humanist typeface Schneidler has fairly inconsistent stroke weights. This makes it relatively sensitive to the bleaching effects of bright-white, gloss-coated papers.

This is dummy text. It is not meant to be read for content, but rather to create an even texture in order to evaluate typefaces more easily. One may, at a glance, quickly judge the 'colour', or grey value, of a typeface using such a text. Then one may check how easily readable a text is and how it affects the reader. One may measure how wide or narrow it sets and, upon closer examination, recognize individual letters and their quirks or special features. As one compares typefaces more and more often, one is eventually able to identify and name them.

# Eight faces
# on four papers

Sans serif and slab serif (Egyptian) on gloss-coated
art paper

A solid sans serif like Frutiger and its many relatives cannot be easily harmed by the brilliance of gloss-coated papers. This holds even more true for matt-coated art papers.

This is dummy text. It is not meant to be read for content, but rather to create an even texture in order to evaluate typefaces more easily. One may, at a glance, quickly judge the 'colour', or grey value, of a typeface using such a text. Then one may check how easily readable a text is and how it affects the reader. One may measure how wide or narrow it sets and, upon closer examination, recognize individual letters and their quirks or special features. As one compares typefaces more and more often, one is eventually able to identify and name them.

Helvetica Semibold, because of the strong contrast, is at risk of appearing blotchy on gloss-coated papers (but not as much as on bright-white copier paper).

**This is dummy text. It is not meant to be read for content, but rather to create an even texture in order to evaluate typefaces more easily. One may, at a glance, quickly judge the 'colour', or grey value, of a typeface using such a text. Then one may check how easily readable a text is and how it affects the reader. One may measure how wide or narrow it sets and, upon closer examination, recognize individual letters and their quirks or special features. As one compares typefaces more and more often, one is eventually able to identify and name them.**

Typefaces like News Gothic are at serious risk of being bleached out on high-gloss papers as much as bright-white papers.

This is dummy text. It is not meant to be read for content, but rather to create an even texture in order to evaluate typefaces more easily. One may, at a glance, quickly judge the 'colour', or grey value, of a typeface using such a text. Then one may check how easily readable a text is and how it affects the reader. One may measure how wide or narrow it sets and, upon closer examination, recognize individual letters and their quirks or special features. As one compares typefaces more and more often, one is eventually able to identify and name them. Of course, this requires attention to detail and practice.

The even and well-balanced slab serif, Rockwell, is stable enough to have no fear of a glossy finish.

This is dummy text. It is not meant to be read for content, but rather to create an even texture in order to evaluate typefaces more easily. One may, at a glance, quickly judge the 'colour', or grey value, of a typeface using such a text. Then one may check how easily readable a text is and how it affects the reader. One may measure how wide or narrow it sets and, upon closer examination, recognize individual letters and their quirks or special features. As one compares typefaces more and more often, one is eventually able to identify and name them.

# Eight faces
# on four papers

### Roman on gloss-coated art paper

Bodoni does not sit well on gloss-coated art papers. Its thin strokes appear even thinner than they really are on such a surface and the thick verticals are excessively stressed. Matt-coated art papers are somewhat better suited, but still not ideal.

This is dummy text. It is not meant to be read for content, but rather to create an even texture in order to evaluate typefaces more easily. One may, at a glance, quickly judge the 'colour', or grey value, of a typeface using such a text. Then one may check how easily readable a text is and how it affects the reader. One may measure how wide or narrow it sets and, upon closer examination, recognize individual letters and their quirks or special features. As one compares typefaces more and more often, one is eventually able to identify and name them.

Garamond has a somewhat reserved relationship with this particular art paper, with its mineral 'coat', but it nonetheless manages to preserve its calm and reader-friendly character.

This is dummy text. It is not meant to be read for content, but rather to create an even texture in order to evaluate typefaces more easily. One may, at a glance, quickly judge the 'colour', or grey value, of a typeface using such a text. Then one may check how easily readable a text is and how it affects the reader. One may measure how wide or narrow it sets and, upon closer examination, recognize individual letters and their quirks or special features. As one compares typefaces more and more often, one is eventually able to identify and name them.

Times Roman doesn't manage to keep the peace with glossy art papers, but appears rather irregular and uneven on the smooth and shiny surface. Even on an off-white glossy, there is too much contrast in the counters.

This is dummy text. It is not meant to be read for content, but rather to create an even texture in order to evaluate typefaces more easily. One may, at a glance, quickly judge the 'colour', or grey value, of a typeface using such a text. Then one may check how easily readable a text is and how it affects the reader. One may measure how wide or narrow it sets and, upon closer examination, recognize individual letters and their quirks or special features. As one compares typefaces more and more often, one is eventually able to identify and name them.

The strokes of Schneidler appear even thinner than they really are on gloss-coated art paper.

This is dummy text. It is not meant to be read for content, but rather to create an even texture in order to evaluate typefaces more easily. One may, at a glance, quickly judge the 'colour', or grey value, of a typeface using such a text. Then one may check how easily readable a text is and how it affects the reader. One may measure how wide or narrow it sets and, upon closer examination, recognize individual letters and their quirks or special features. As one compares typefaces more and more often, one is eventually able to identify and name them.

# 5

# Eight faces
# on four papers

Bodoni manages quite well on this off-white lightly calendered offset paper. Giambattista Bodoni himself demanded such paper in the 18th century so that his typefaces would appear crisp and precise.

This is dummy text. It is not meant to be read for content, but rather to create an even texture in order to evaluate typefaces more easily. One may, at a glance, quickly judge the 'colour', or grey value, of a typeface using such a text. Then one may check how easily readable a text is and how it affects the reader. One may measure how wide or narrow it sets and, upon closer examination, recognize individual letters and their quirks or special features. As one compares typefaces more and more often, one is eventually able to identify and name them.

Garamond is impeccable on a calendered offset although it would prefer a somewhat rougher surface.

This is dummy text. It is not meant to be read for content, but rather to create an even texture in order to evaluate typefaces more easily. One may, at a glance, quickly judge the 'colour', or grey value, of a typeface using such a text. Then one may check how easily readable a text is and how it affects the reader. One may measure how wide or narrow it sets and, upon closer examination, recognize individual letters and their quirks or special features. As one compares typefaces more and more often, one is eventually able to identify and name them.

Times Roman confirms its reputation as a hard-wearing typeface on this type of paper.

This is dummy text. It is not meant to be read for content, but rather to create an even texture in order to evaluate typefaces more easily. One may, at a glance, quickly judge the 'colour', or grey value, of a typeface using such a text. Then one may check how easily readable a text is and how it affects the reader. One may measure how wide or narrow it sets and, upon closer examination, recognize individual letters and their quirks or special features. As one compares typefaces more and more often, one is eventually able to identify and name them.

Schneidler also has no difficulties on a calendered offset paper.

This is dummy text. It is not meant to be read for content, but rather to create an even texture in order to evaluate typefaces more easily. One may, at a glance, quickly judge the 'colour', or grey value, of a typeface using such a text. Then one may check how easily readable a text is and how it affects the reader. One may measure how wide or narrow it sets and, upon closer examination, recognize individual letters and their quirks or special features. As one compares typefaces more and more often, one is eventually able to identify and name them.

# 6

# Eight faces
# on four papers

On offset paper with a surface closed through light calendering, sans serifs and slab serifs appear precise and retain good legibility, as long as the paper is not too white. This is demonstrated here with Frutiger, Helvetica SemiBold, News Gothic and Rockwell.

To summarize:
• When text and image are of equal importance, a lightly calendered offset paper is the right choice.

• When quality of the images is a prime concern, gloss-coated (and expensive) art paper is appropriate.

• When reading long texts is the primary goal, or when smaller type is required, book paper (or antique wove) is the most suitable.

In every case, typeface and paper must be chosen to complement each other.

This is dummy text. It is not meant to be read for content, but rather to create an even texture in order to evaluate typefaces more easily. One may, at a glance, quickly judge the 'colour', or grey value, of a typeface using such a text. Then one may check how easily readable a text is and how it affects the reader. One may measure how wide or narrow it sets and, upon closer examination, recognize individual letters and their quirks or special features. As one compares typefaces more and more often, one is eventually able to identify and name them.

**This is dummy text. It is not meant to be read for content, but rather to create an even texture in order to evaluate typefaces more easily. One may, at a glance, quickly judge the 'colour', or grey value, of a typeface using such a text. Then one may check how easily readable a text is and how it affects the reader. One may measure how wide or narrow it sets and, upon closer examination, recognize individual letters and their quirks or special features. As one compares typefaces more and more often, one is eventually able to identify and name them.**

This is dummy text. It is not meant to be read for content, but rather to create an even texture in order to evaluate typefaces more easily. One may, at a glance, quickly judge the 'colour', or grey value, of a typeface using such a text. Then one may check how easily readable a text is and how it affects the reader. One may measure how wide or narrow it sets and, upon closer examination, recognize individual letters and their quirks or special features. As one compares typefaces more and more often, one is eventually able to identify and name them. Of course, this requires attention to detail and practice.

This is dummy text. It is not meant to be read for content, but rather to create an even texture in order to evaluate typefaces more easily. One may, at a glance, quickly judge the 'colour', or grey value, of a typeface using such a text. Then one may check how easily readable a text is and how it affects the reader. One may measure how wide or narrow it sets and, upon closer examination, recognize individual letters and their quirks or special features. As one compares typefaces more and more often, one is eventually able to identify and name them.

# 7

# Eight faces
# on four papers

### Roman on book paper

Bodoni feels quite at home on book paper (also known as 'antique wove') with its off-white colour and its somewhat rougher surface. It has a calming, and thereby reader-friendly, effect.

This is dummy text. It is not meant to be read for content, but rather to create an even texture in order to evaluate typefaces more easily. One may, at a glance, quickly judge the 'colour', or grey value, of a typeface using such a text. Then one may check how easily readable a text is and how it affects the reader. One may measure how wide or narrow it sets and, upon closer examination, recognize individual letters and their quirks or special features. As one compares typefaces more and more often, one is eventually able to identify and name them.

The soft shade and coarse feel of book paper suit Garamond well. At the time of its origin in the 16th century it was printed on rag paper, which had a vaguely comparable quality.

This is dummy text. It is not meant to be read for content, but rather to create an even texture in order to evaluate typefaces more easily. One may, at a glance, quickly judge the 'colour', or grey value, of a typeface using such a text. Then one may check how easily readable a text is and how it affects the reader. One may measure how wide or narrow it sets and, upon closer examination, recognize individual letters and their quirks or special features. As one compares typefaces more and more often, one is eventually able to identify and name them.

Times Roman appears calm and reader-friendly on book paper; the letterforms have a better combination with this than with other papers.

This is dummy text. It is not meant to be read for content, but rather to create an even texture in order to evaluate typefaces more easily. One may, at a glance, quickly judge the 'colour', or grey value, of a typeface using such a text. Then one may check how easily readable a text is and how it affects the reader. One may measure how wide or narrow it sets and, upon closer examination, recognize individual letters and their quirks or special features. As one compares typefaces more and more often, one is eventually able to identify and name them.

Schneidler works well on most papers, but especially well on book paper.

This is dummy text. It is not meant to be read for content, but rather to create an even texture in order to evaluate typefaces more easily. One may, at a glance, quickly judge the 'colour', or grey value, of a typeface using such a text. Then one may check how easily readable a text is and how it affects the reader. One may measure how wide or narrow it sets and, upon closer examination, recognize individual letters and their quirks or special features. As one compares typefaces more and more often, one is eventually able to identify and name them.

# 8

# Eight faces
# on four papers

Book paper, with its off-white shading and slightly rough finish, agrees with just about any typeface, including Frutiger.

This is dummy text. It is not meant to be read for content, but rather to create an even texture in order to evaluate typefaces more easily. One may, at a glance, quickly judge the 'colour', or grey value, of a typeface using such a text. Then one may check how easily readable a text is and how it affects the reader. One may measure how wide or narrow it sets and, upon closer examination, recognize individual letters and their quirks or special features. As one compares typefaces more and more often, one is eventually able to identify and name them.

When the black and white contrast is reduced through the slight tinting of this paper, Helvetica Semibold is in less danger of becoming blotchy on the page. The lines become comfortable stripes.

**This is dummy text. It is not meant to be read for content, but rather to create an even texture in order to evaluate typefaces more easily. One may, at a glance, quickly judge the 'colour', or grey value, of a typeface using such a text. Then one may check how easily readable a text is and how it affects the reader. One may measure how wide or narrow it sets and, upon closer examination, recognize individual letters and their quirks or special features. As one compares typefaces more and more often, one is eventually able to identify and name them.**

This off-white paper doesn't bleach out the fine strokes of News Gothic; the danger of flicker is therefore warded off.

This is dummy text. It is not meant to be read for content, but rather to create an even texture in order to evaluate typefaces more easily. One may, at a glance, quickly judge the 'colour', or grey value, of a typeface using such a text. Then one may check how easily readable a text is and how it affects the reader. One may measure how wide or narrow it sets and, upon closer examination, recognize individual letters and their quirks or special features. As one compares typefaces more and more often, one is eventually able to identify and name them. Of course, this requires attention to detail and practice.

Rockwell can be easily read without effort or irritation on antique wove. This also holds true for its lighter or bolder slab-serif relatives.

This is dummy text. It is not meant to be read for content, but rather to create an even texture in order to evaluate typefaces more easily. One may, at a glance, quickly judge the 'colour', or grey value, of a typeface using such a text. Then one may check how easily readable a text is and how it affects the reader. One may measure how wide or narrow it sets and, upon closer examination, recognize individual letters and their quirks or special features. As one compares typefaces more and more often, one is eventually able to identify and name them.

# Repro, printing, paper and legibility

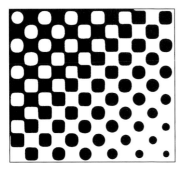

Just as type and paper must fit together, the printing process also has to be considered. In order to print grey tones, images have to be broken up into tiny points of black (halftone dots). Resolutions range from 55 dots per inch for newsprint to 300 dots per inch for finest art paper. In the lightest parts of an image, the halftone dots are small and 'sharp'; the darker the area, the larger the halftone dots become, until they close up completely at solid black.

Different paper surfaces take up the printing inks in different ways. The halftone dots stay clean on papers with a closed surface. With rougher, more absorbent papers, the ink soaks in and spreads, so the halftone dots become larger (dot gain). This must be taken into consideration during the creation of litho plates for printing.

These examples demonstrate the various printing techniques (reproduced, of course), in each case enlarged and at actual size.

## Printing

This is dummy text. It is not meant to be read for content, but rather to create an even texture in order to evaluate typefaces more easily. One may, at a glance, quickly judge the 'colour', or grey value, of a typeface using such a text.

Then one may check how easily readable a text is and how it affects the reader. One may measure how wide or narrow it sets and, upon closer examination, recognize individual letters and their quirks or special features. As one compares typefaces more and more often, one is eventually able to identify and name them.

Offset printing.
This process is mainly used to print large sheets of paper or board, for long runs. The type image is clean and even. Most of today's typefaces are made for this printing process.

## Printing

This is dummy text. It is not meant to be read for content, but rather to create an even texture in order to evaluate typefaces more easily. One may, at a glance, quickly judge the 'colour', or grey value, of a typeface using such a text.

Then one may check how easily readable a text is and how it affects the reader. One may measure how wide or narrow it sets and, upon closer examination, recognize individual letters and their quirks or special features. As one compares typefaces more and more often, one is eventually able to identify and name them.

Photocopied type.
This method is used as a quick reproduction system to transfer text or images onto paper. The quality of photocopied type varies enormously, therefore typefaces in small sizes must be carefully chosen as the reproduction of fine serifs can sometimes be lost.

## Printing

This is dummy text. It is not meant to be read for content, but rather to create an even texture in order to evaluate typefaces more easily. One may, at a glance, quickly judge the 'colour', or grey value, of a typeface using such a text.

Then one may check how easily readable a text is and how it affects the reader. One may measure how wide or narrow it sets and, upon closer examination, recognize individual letters and their quirks or special features. As one compares typefaces more and more often, one is eventually able to identify and name them.

Laser printer.
The example shows computer output with a 600 dpi laser printer. The type image is softer and somewhat heavier than with offset printing. One can recognize the resultant 'jaggies' in the enlargement.

## Printing

This is dummy text. It is not meant to be read for content, but rather to create an even texture in order to evaluate typefaces more easily. One may, at a glance, quickly judge the 'colour', or grey value, of a typeface using such a text.

Then one may check how easily readable a text is and how it affects the reader. One may measure how wide or narrow it sets and, upon closer examination, recognize individual letters and their quirks or special features. As one compares typefaces more and more often, one is eventually able to identify and name them.

Ink-jet printer.
This is computer output with an ink-jet printer. The ink is absorbed by the paper, giving a spongy effect.

## Printing

This is dummy text. It is not meant to be read for content, but rather to create an even texture in order to evaluate typefaces more easily. One may, at a glance, quickly judge the 'colour', or grey value, of a typeface using such a text.

Then one may check how easily readable a text is and how it affects the reader. One may measure how wide or narrow it sets and, upon closer examination, recognize individual letters and their quirks or special features. As one compares typefaces more and more often, one is eventually able to identify and name them.

Faxed type.
Typefaces and sizes must be carefully chosen to guarantee legibility in spite of the abuses of this reproduction technique.

# Typography: binding and reading

One of life's unwritten laws: your destination is always exactly at the spot at which the road map won't quite open.

What is done last must be considered first: the bookbinding work. When designers don't consider how a piece of work will be folded, trimmed and glued, they can make an error of judgement in dealing with the typography. Again, it goes without saying that it is vital to establish a good working relationship with printers and bookbinders.

## Gluing

The pages of a book – whether it is a booklet of 48 pages or a thicker volume – must be glued together at the back. Different glue types have various effects on the flexibility of the binding and allow pages to lie flat to different degrees. This must be taken into account in typographic design.

With the use of hot-melt glue, one should leave at least 14mm ($\frac{1}{2}$ inch to $\frac{5}{8}$ inch) back margin (space between the inner edge of the page and the type area). Use of a more elastic dispersion glue needs only 10mm ($\frac{3}{8}$ inch).

Card-weight covers and end papers are glued to the first page of a section, taking 3–5mm ($\frac{1}{8}$ – $\frac{3}{16}$ inch) space. One must take this into account in the design of the first page.

If you can't open the bus timetable fully, you won't know that the bus has already gone.

| | | | | | | | |
|---|---|---|---|---|---|---|---|
| - Bergstraße | 12.42 | 13.32 | 14.47 | 16.03 | 17.29 | 18.47 | 19.33 |
| - Gewerbegebiet | 12.43 | 13.33 | 14.48 | 16.04 | 17.30 | 18.48 | 19.34 |
| Klein-Linden Waldweide | | 13.35 | | | | | |
| - Wetzlarer Straße | 12.48 | 13.39 | 14.51 | | 17.35 | 18.51 | |
| Gießen Robert-Sommer-Straße | 12.49 | 13.40 | 14.53 | | 17.36 | 18.53 | |
| - Klinikstraße | 12.50 | 13.41 | 14.55 | | 17.37 | 18.55 | |
| - Friedrichstraße | 12.52 | 13.44 | 14.57 | | 17.39 | 18.57 | |
| - Liebigstraße | 12.53 | 13.45 | 14.58 | | 17.40 | 18.58 | |
| - Berliner Platz | 12.54 | 13.46 | 14.59 | | 17.41 | 18.59 | |
| - Johanneskirche | | | | | | | |
| Bahnhof | 13.00 | 13.52 | 15.05 | 16.15 | 17.47 | 19.05 | 19.45 |

**33** 5101 Rundverkehr Gießen → Lin

REGIONALVERKEHR KURHE

| Verkehrsbeschränkungen | | | | F | S | | Montag - Frei<br>S |
|---|---|---|---|---|---|---|---|
| Gießen Johanneskirche | | | | | | | |
| - Bahnhof | 5.00 | 5.50 | 6.15 | 6.50 | 6.50 | | 7.30 |
| - Friedrichstraße | 5.03 | 5.53 | 6.17 | 6.53 | 6.53 | | 7.33 |
| - Klinikstraße | 5.04 | 5.54 | 6.18 | 6.54 | 6.54 | | 7.34 |
| - Robert-Sommer-Straße | 5.06 | 5.56 | 6.20 | 6.56 | 6.56 | | 7.36 |
| Klein-Linden Wetzlarer Straße | 5.07 | 5.57 | 6.21 | 6.57 | 6.57 | | 7.37 |
| - Waldweide | 5.09 | 5.59 | 6.23 | 6.59 | 6.59 | | 7.39 |

## Creep

Paper has volume: there are thicker and thinner, lighter and heavier stocks. When a large sheet of paper is folded into a section of 8, 16 or even 32 pages, the open edge is not even; rather, the inner 'quires' stick out by an amount roughly equal to their thickness. The thicker the paper, the greater the difference in breadth. A printed piece may be made up of several such sections which are organized and sequenced through the use of a 'signature' on the first page of each section. These are all eventually trimmed to the same width.

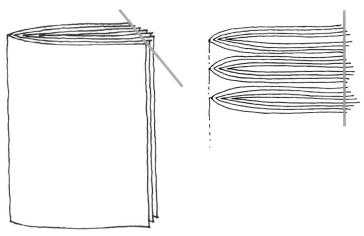

Paper creep with one or more sections. The gold line shows the trim.

This of course has consequences and designers need to be aware of it. Margins around columns, for example, will be larger on outer pages than on inner pages. While graphic designers should not adjust the grid spread by spread, it is important to ensure that you leave sufficient margins, so that when the pages are trimmed nothing ends up too close to the outer edge of the page.

### Trimming

It is not technically possible to trim the entire print run of a printed piece precisely to the millimetre. All page elements (images, shaded surfaces, rules etc) which are intended to run to the edge of the page need to be given a 3mm (⅛ inch) 'bleed'.

On one page, the thumb index has lots of room; a few pages later, it's threatened by the trim.

The page numbers dance through the whole book. To avoid this, the typographer should ensure that type is not positioned too close to the bottom of the page.

### Folding differences and the effects of trim

Folding not only influences the width of the pages, but it can affect the page depth as well. If titles are placed too near the top and folios too near the bottom, there is a danger that folding and trimming differences will become too obvious as the two examples on the opposite page show. This is especially true for rules that run across double-page spreads.

Heading

Correct.

Heading

Incorrect.

The left-hand page.
How the typographer planned it.
The right-hand page.
Trim differences weren't considered as the right margin is now narrower than the left.

Heading

Correct.

Heading

Incorrect.

The left-hand page.
This is how the typographer planned it.
The right-hand page.
This is how it turned out. The folio is too close to the bottom of the page and consequently there is too much space at the top. Trim differences weren't considered.

Stitching of a section through the back of folded sheets.

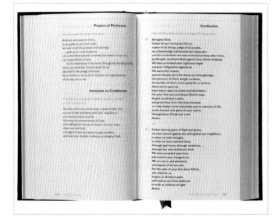

Hardback stitched book.

## Binding and typography

Whether a printed piece is stitched or bound, it is important to bear the binding method in mind. Binding is the last stage of production but must be one of the first considerations in the planning.

The simplest method is stitching, either with wire (saddle-stitching) for thinner documents or – more expensive – with thread (sewn binding). The quantity of pages that may be bound with this method depends on the weight of the paper; heavy book paper may limit a book to 32 pages. With sewn binding, sections are sewn, glued and bound in paper or with a hard cover.

Paperbacks have the cover glued directly onto assembled pages which can result in creasing or breaking the back of the book when it is opened. This does not occur with hard covers as the back of the spine remains hollow. This is good for flexibility and durability but demands a more complicated (and expensive) construction. Both processes have many variations, all of which have their effects on the design. This is why advance planning is so important.

Paperback binding often uses scoring to ensure that the cover can be turned. The score is created by pressing heavyweight paper or lightweight board between two metal surfaces, one with a raised metal rule and the other with a recessed groove. This process allows for the fibres in the paper or board to be compressed, creating a hinge.

With 'perfect binding', which is often used for thicker magazines or directories and paperback novels, the backs are milled and then glued together. This is used for publications with a short life span as the glue often becomes brittle and over time can break.

Spiral binding allows a publication to open flat and stay flat. It is generally only used for published material with a low page extent and has the disadvantage of poor alignment between pages.

Spiral binding allows the pages to open fully.

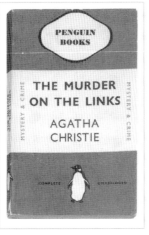

Paperback binding with
two 'scores' or grooves.

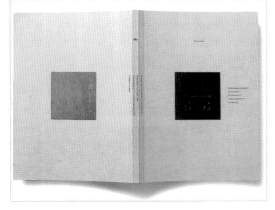

Paperback binding with four 'scores' is more durable
but those on the front and back must be taken into
account by the designer.

Apparently this designer was not
informed about the scoring.

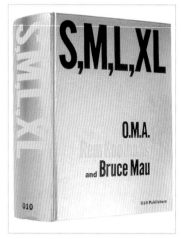
Hardback book with embossed typography.

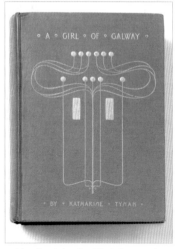
Hardback book with foil stamping.

## Hard cover

The technical requirements of hard-cover publications have a greater influence on the typographic design than paperbacks. A book is a three-dimensional object; this must be taken into account.

Fold joints must be considered when designing the binding cover, in order that parts of illustrations, photographs or text do not sink into the furrow. Various materials are suited for use in covering hard bindings:
• imitation cloth
• real cloth
• leather
• vinyl
• plastic

All materials have their special characteristics; some are appropriate only for embossing or offset printing. This of course affects the design.

When the cover design has to include print effects such as foil-stamping or embossing, one must consider the thickness of the cover material. It is also vital that the embossing or stamping does not run to the edges of the cover or over scores. This is not a problem with printed book covers.

# Typography on screen

When we speak of 'typography', we usually imagine text printed on paper. However, more and more text is read on screens. Most of what applies to paper also applies to the screen, but there are a few extra snares in this area to be aware of.

Type on paper is stable – it is committed there, whether good or bad, once and for all. Type on screen can be unstable. With regard to the Internet, designers have the particular problem that the designer cannot control the end user's view of a web page. This is due to differences in screen size, colours, operating systems and browsers. There is of course another factor to contend with, and that is multiple-platform publishing on screen, where content is designed to be viewed across websites, CD-ROMs, mobile phones, PDAs, ebooks etc. Because of the complexity of the subject, this section merely covers the basic principles and gives you, the reader, the starting point for further investigation.

Type on screen can cause letterforms to appear lighter or darker, more blurred or sharper than their printed counterparts. Screen type is also non-static: the viewer has to scroll to view text rather than turning a page. In an environment where everything is movable the designer has to maintain as much control of the type as possible in order to maximize readability.

One important point to remember, for webpage design in particular, is that the attention span of the viewer is far shorter than that of someone reading a book or magazine. When reading from a screen the viewer takes 10 to 20 percent longer to read the same printed material; therefore it is vital that the text is well considered in terms of detail and composition as well as the effectiveness of its communication.

The chief mistakes made in conventional screen typography:
- lines too long;
- type too small;
- poorly readable typeface;
- too much text;
- bad line breaks;
- poor colour combinations;
- text over unsuitable backgrounds.

## Colour of type

When dealing with type, 'colour' refers to the overall tone of letterforms or a block of text on a page.

The following examples demonstrate how important it is to have adequate contrast when using type on a screen.

This is dummy text. It is not meant to be read for content, but rather to create an even texture in order to evaluate typefaces more easily. One may, at a glance, quickly judge the 'colour', or grey value, of a typeface using such a text. Then one may check how easily readable a text is and how it affects the reader. One may measure how wide or narrow it sets and upon closer examination, recognize individual letters and their quirks or special features. As one compares typefaces more and more often, one is eventually able to identify and name them. Of course, this requires attention to detail and practice.

Normal type on a light background, as long as it is well set, is clearly readable.

This is dummy text. It is not meant to be read for content, but rather to create an even texture in order to evaluate typefaces more easily. One may, at a glance, quickly judge the 'colour', or grey value, of a typeface using such a text. Then one may check how easily readable a text is and how it affects the reader. One may measure how wide or narrow it sets and upon closer examination, recognize individual letters and their quirks or special features. As one compares typefaces more and more often, one is eventually able to identify and name them. Of course, this requires attention to detail and practice.

A heavier typeface is better able to assert itself in an unfriendly environment.

These examples are set in tones of black on white. However, the use of colour is a popular option with many designers who work on screen as the cost constraints that print designers are faced with are not relevant. When designers use colours for backgrounds and type there can be issues with contrast, as the two can blur into one another. As such, use high-contrast colours for background and type to ensure that the type is as legible as possible; of course using black and white ensures the highest possible contrast and good readability.

This is dummy text. It is not meant to be read for content, but rather to create an even texture in order to evaluate typefaces more easily. One may, at a glance, quickly judge the 'colour', or grey value, of a typeface using such a text. Then one may check how easily readable a text is and how it affects the reader. One may measure how wide or narrow it sets and upon closer examination, recognize individual letters and their quirks or special features. As one compares typefaces more and more often, one is eventually able to identify and name them. Of course, this requires attention to detail and practice.

The same type on a darker background has a more difficult time of it.

Colour is frequently used for hyperlinks within websites. Here coloured text can indicate that the link is to be clicked, changing colour once it has been visited.

## Typography for the screen

Screen typography must not be too thin. Letters running together should be avoided, as must typefaces with easily confused letterforms.

Serif typefaces are often used in print for large blocks of text as they are easy to read. Times is a popular choice but was originally designed to be used in newspaper design where many letterforms were squeezed together to maximize space, whilst still maintaining legibility. On screen, however, the thin serifs do not render well, as the subtleties of the serifs and ascenders and descenders do not translate successfully into a pixel form. In print, a small serif is a small serif; on screen, the pixel translates the small serif into a larger, thicker serif with visual noise.

Most typefaces used on screen are not designed to be legible but mimic their print counterparts. At present it is therefore preferable to use sans-serif typefaces, which are far better for our low-resolution screens. (This advice will change as screen resolutions improve.)

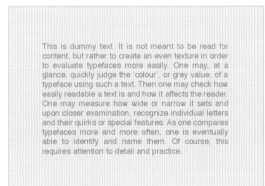

This example demonstrates how tones merge.

This is dummy text. It is not meant to be read for content, but rather to create an even texture in order to evaluate typefaces more easily. One may, at a glance, quickly judge the 'colour', or grey value, of a typeface using such a text. Then one may check how easily readable a text is and how it affects the reader. One may measure how wide or narrow it sets and upon closer examination, recognize individual letters and their quirks or special features. As one compares typefaces more and more often, one is eventually able to identify and name them. Of course, this requires attention to detail and practice.

Black and white is a high-contrast solution. However, there can be problems with legibility of type if the typeface choice is too light.

Compare Verdana to Arial and Georgia to Times. The individual letterforms in Arial and Times do not have such considered spacing for screen legibility as Verdana and Georgia. Watch out for pixels within letters, in particular a, o, e, closing together and when serifs merge into each other. This causes problems with readability and can be tiring for the viewer.

Verdana (sans serif) and Georgia (serif), designed by Matthew Carter for Microsoft, have been specifially created to work with the natural pixel grid, with their shape and letterspacing optimized for legibility on screen. They therefore work well on a web page but do not transfer well to paper, due to the high resolution of the medium and the large x-heights and heavy letterforms.

Verdana has been designed with a large x-height, open counters and clear letterforms (Jj Ll, Ii, 1), and has extra space between the characters producing loose, even text with good readability.

Georgia has a larger x-height than other serif typefaces (such as Times) ensuring that it is clear and easy to read on screen.

This is dummy text. It is not meant to be read for content, but rather to create an even texture in order to evaluate typefaces more easily. One may, at a glance, quickly judge the 'colour', or grey value, of a typeface using such a text. Then one may check how easily readable a text is and how it affects the reader. One may measure how wide or narrow it sets and upon closer examination, recognize individual letters and their quirks or special features. As one compares typefaces more and more often, one is eventually able to identify and name them.

Verdana.

This is dummy text. It is not meant to be read for content, but rather to create an even texture in order to evaluate typefaces more easily. One may, at a glance, quickly judge the 'colour', or grey value, of a typeface using such a text. Then one may check how easily readable a text is and how it affects the reader. One may measure how wide or narrow it sets and upon closer examination, recognize individual letters and their quirks or special features. As one compares typefaces more and more often, one is eventually able to identify and name them. Of course, this requires attention to detail and practice.

Georgia.

This is dummy text. It is not meant to be read for content, but rather to create an even texture in order to evaluate typefaces more easily. One may, at a glance, quickly judge the 'colour', or grey value, of a typeface using such a text. Then one may check how easily readable a text is and how it affects the reader. One may measure how wide or narrow it sets and upon closer examination, recognize individual letters and their quirks or special features. As one compares typefaces more and more often, one is eventually able to identify and name them. Of course, this requires attention to detail and practice.

Arial.

This is dummy text. It is not meant to be read for content, but rather to create an even texture in order to evaluate typefaces more easily. One may, at a glance, quickly judge the 'colour', or grey value, of a typeface using such a text. Then one may check how easily readable a text is and how it affects the reader. One may measure how wide or narrow it sets and upon closer examination, recognize individual letters and their quirks or special features. As one compares typefaces more and more often, one is eventually able to identify and name them. Of course, this requires attention to detail and practice.

Times.

Note that Monotype offers 'Enhanced Screen Quality' typefaces, which include Arial, Century Schoolbook, Impact, LetterGothic and Nimrod.

## Typography for the Internet

When using HTML and selecting fonts for designing web pages, designers have to be aware that even though they have specified a particular typeface the users may not have it installed on their computers. In this case the browser will defer to a list of typefaces written within the HTML code to find one available on the user's computer.

Another point to note is that most screen typefaces are displayed with little leading in a browser. It is as important to control the leading (in relation to a chosen typeface and its x-height) when working on screen as in print.

The two examples on this page show how rules for leading in printed type needed to be adjusted for viewing on screen.

This is dummy text. It is not meant to be read for content, but rather to create an even texture in order to evaluate typefaces more easily. One may, at a glance, quickly judge the 'colour', or grey value, of a typeface using such a text. Then one may check how easily readable a text is and how it affects the reader. One may measure how wide or narrow it sets and upon closer examination, recognize individual letters and their quirks or special features. As one compares typefaces more and more often, one is eventually able to identify and name them. Of course, this requires attention to detail and practice.

The leading shown here would normally be acceptable for a print solution but it has been used on screen.

This is dummy text. It is not meant to be read for content, but rather to create an even texture in order to evaluate typefaces more easily. One may, at a glance, quickly judge the 'colour', or grey value, of a typeface using such a text. Then one may check how easily readable a text is and how it affects the reader. One may measure how wide or narrow it sets and upon closer examination, recognize individual letters and their quirks or special features. As one compares typefaces more and more often, one is eventually able to identify and name them. Of course, this requires attention to detail and practice.

The same typeface but with more generous leading for screen use.

## Line lengths, leading and scrolling

Designers will often give thought to the choice of typeface and typesize on screen but beyond that they exert no further control. Often text is simply 'poured' onto pages, flowing to the document width with no consideration being given to the line length, the line breaks or the space surrounding it.

Line lengths are invariably too long, resulting in difficulty in turning from one line to another. Reading on screen is strenuous. Hence one should oblige the reader with lines of no more than 50–55 characters.

The two examples on this page illustrate good and bad line lengths.

This is dummy text. It is not meant to be read for content, but rather to create an even texture in order to evaluate typefaces more easily. One may, at a glance, quickly judge the 'colour', or grey value, of a typeface using such a text. Then one may check how easily readable a text is and how it affects the reader. One may measure how wide or narrow it sets and upon closer examination, recognize individual letters and their quirks or special features. As one compares typefaces more and more often, one is eventually able to identify and name them. Of course, this requires attention to detail and practice.

Lines are too long, type is too small and too close to the document edge. You can fit a lot on the screen but readability suffers greatly.

This is dummy text. It is not meant to be read for content, but rather to create an even texture in order to evaluate typefaces more easily. One may, at a glance, quickly judge the 'colour', or grey value, of a typeface using such a text. Then one may check how easily readable a text is and how it affects the reader. One may measure how wide or narrow it sets and upon closer examination, recognize individual letters and their quirks or special features.

Here the size is larger, the lines shorter, concentrated in the middle, resulting in better readability.

When lines are shorter, leading has to be increased. (Consequently wordspacing should not be too tight.) Indeed, where leading is increased considerably (up to 130 percent in some cases) the viewer will notice a vast improvement with regard to readability.

Horizontal scrolling can be a problem as often the viewer doesn't notice the scroll bar and misses part of the content. Avoid horizontal scrolling at 800 x 600 (monitor resolution).

If there is a lot of text the viewer will have to scroll vertically down the page, which can be laborious and tiring when trying to read. Consider breaking up the information into smaller chunks and link some of this text to other pages. If the text has to be together, ensure that there is adequate paragraph spacing to give the reader a visual break.

This is dummy text.
It is not meant to be read for content,
but rather to create an even texture
in order to evaluate typefaces more easily.
One may, at a glance, quickly judge the
'colour', or grey value, of a typeface
using such a text.
Then one may check how easily readable
a text is and how it affects the reader.
One may measure how wide or
narrow it sets.

The example here shows open wordspacing with extra leading and short line length.

This is dummy text. It is not meant to be read for content, but ra
to create an even texture in order to evaluate typefaces n
easily. One may, at a glance, quickly judge the 'colour', or g
value, of a typeface using such a text. Then one may check
easily readable a text is and how it affects the reader. One
measure how wide or narrow it sets and upon closer examinat
recognize individual letters and their quirks or special features
one compares typefaces more and more often, one is eventu
able to identify and name them. Of course, this requires attentio
detail and practice.

This example shows how information can be missed.

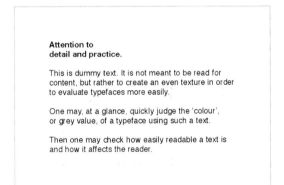

**Attention to detail
and practice.**
This is dummy text. It is not meant to be read for
content, but rather to create an even texture in order
to evaluate typefaces more easily. One may, at a
glance, quickly judge the 'colour', or grey value, of a
typeface using such a text. Then one may check how
easily readable a text is and how it affects the reader.

Line and word breaks should be made according to
meaning. The above example is wrong.

**Attention to
detail and practice.**

This is dummy text. It is not meant to be read for
content, but rather to create an even texture in order
to evaluate typefaces more easily.

One may, at a glance, quickly judge the 'colour',
or grey value, of a typeface using such a text.

Then one may check how easily readable a text is
and how it affects the reader.

In this example the line and word breaks have been
made with consideration for the meaning.

## Hierarchy of text

To facilitate the search for information on screen, material needs to be structured in a logical manner and be easy to navigate. It is necessary to construct the information in such a way that it can be viewed in small and digestible chunks – a hierarchy.

The information should be approached in a way similar to a piece of print. For example, what is the sequence that the viewer will follow when visiting the website? What type will the viewer see first and where will it be?

The home page is vital. The arrangement of type can either attract the viewer to look at more of the site or not. The most vital elements should be placed 'above the fold', which is the first screen viewed without having to scroll. If elements have to be placed below the fold, ensure the viewer has some indication of this.

Another way to ensure quick navigation through a block of text or on a page is to add emphasis. This is usually done through the use of weights, mainly normal (roman) or bold. Light is not usually an option as strokes cannot be thinner than one pixel. Although italics are used in printed material it is not advisable to use them on screen as they cause pixelation and do not work well with the pixel grid, especially when used at a small scale. Underlining is used frequently in web design as it indicates a hypertext link.

Difference in weight and emphasis can also be created through colour and tone. However, a word of caution: the more colours the designer uses, the more emphasis is created and the more confusing the design.

Information needs a clear demarcation from its background. A line of small type on an empty page will dominate. When the same text is used on a page full of larger type it will be lost. Space can be used to add emphasis; in books, margins serve this purpose. Type in graphics, tables, captions etc should be ranged left with clear line breaks according to meaning.

# 5

# Additional information

# Additional technical terminology

The technical terminology of typesetting and typography can be found within this section, but also within the relevant chapters:
chapter 1, p.12;
chapter 2, p.59;
chapter 3, p.100;
chapter 4, p.133.

Most terms have been used within the text; there are also a few that have not, but which might nonetheless come in handy.

alignment
1. The vertical edge of a column of text whether justified or not.
2. How characters sit on the baseline.

axis
The line on which the letterform rotates.

blackletter
Typefaces that are based upon Gothic, medieval script.

body type
Type used for main text; also referred to as text type.

bullet
A special character or dot used to indicate a list showing individual but related points.

chase
A metal frame locking metal type as pages ready for printing.

colophon
1. A printer's mark.
2. A description of how a book was produced.

composition
Assembling type into words, sentences, paragraphs and pages.

contrast
In typefaces, the term used to describe differences between stroke thicknesses within characters.

cursive
Letters often associated with italics and which have a flow similar to handwriting.

depth
The vertical depth of a block of print on a page.

display type
Type used for headlines and set larger than the surrounding body type.

em
A unit of measurement, nominally equal to the width of a capital letterform and equal to 12 points.

en
A unit of measurement equal to half an em.

endnote
A piece of text like a footnote but placed at the end of a section, chapter or book.

format
The shape and size of a job.

formatting
To apply a set of instructions to text which then alters its appearance.

Gothic
A term of type classification, sometimes referring to blackletter.

Grotesk
A term for letters without serifs.

head
The blank space at the top of a page.

legibility
The clarity of an alphabet or individual characters.

**Linotype**
The original hot-metal system, founded in 1889, by which a line of type was set at a time.

**macrotypography**
Typographic decisions made with regard to page format and layout, column widths and margins.

**measure**
An alternative term for line length.

**microtypography**
The finer typographic decisions made with regard to letter-, word- and line-spacing.

**minuscules**
In calligraphy, an alternative term for lowercase letters.

**Monotype**
A system of mechanical composition or typesetting machine which casts characters as separate elements.

**pagination**
Organizing the parts of a document into pages.

**point size**
The unit in which size of type is measured (usually 72 points to an inch). It refers to the body of the type (and not the character).

**readability**
How easily or badly a piece of typography can be read when arranged and set in a particular typeface.

**recto**
Right-hand page; takes an odd page number.

**register**
1. The exact lining up of printed matter on both sides of a sheet of paper.
2. The accurate positioning of colour-components in printed matter.

**resolution**
For outputs, lines per inch.
For scanning, dots per inch.

**reversed out of**
Light or white-coloured text on a dark or black background.

**Roman numerals**
i I, ii II, iii III, iv IV, v V, etc.

**rule**
A thin line, whether vertical or horizontal.

**stone**
A flat surface where metal type was laid prior to being locked up in a chase ready for printing.

**stress**
The angle of thickening within a curved letterform.

**stroke-weight**
The thickness of the main lines of letterforms.

**tail**
The bottom of a book page.

**Unicode**
An international standard representing all possible character sets for typesetting.

**verso**
Left-hand page; takes an even page number.

**word images**
Word shapes created by their varying letterforms – whether they have ascenders or descenders, are round or straight etc.

# Appendix 1:
# British and US Macintosh keyboard shortcuts

The following shows characters that are available for most typefaces on a Macintosh keyboard. To find which characters are available in a specific font, search in key caps under the Apple menu.

## Accented characters

| | | | | | |
|---|---|---|---|---|---|
| Å | shift alt | A | ö | alt U | O |
| å | alt | A | Ø | shift alt O | |
| Á | alt E | shift A | ø | alt O | |
| á | alt E | A | Õ | alt N | shift O |
| À | alt ~` | shift A | õ | alt N | O |
| à | alt ~` | A | Ú | alt E | shift U |
| Â | alt I | shift A | ú | alt E | U |
| â | alt I | A | Ù | alt ~` | shift U |
| Ä | alt U | shift A | ù | alt ~` | U |
| ä | alt U | A | Û | alt I | shift U |
| Ã | alt N | shift A | û | alt I | U |
| ã | alt N | A | Ü | alt U | shift U |
| Ç | shift alt C | | ü | alt U | U |
| ç | alt C | | Ÿ | alt U | shift Y |
| É | alt E | shift E | ÿ | alt U | Y |
| é | alt E | E | | | |
| È | alt ~` | shift E | | | |
| è | alt ~` | E | | | |
| Ê | alt I | shift E | | | |
| ê | alt I | E | | | |
| Ë | alt U | shift E | | | |
| ë | alt U | E | | | |
| Í | alt E | shift I | | | |
| í | alt E | I | | | |
| Ì | alt ~` | shift I | | | |
| ì | alt ~` | I | | | |
| Î | alt I | shift I | | | |
| î | alt I | I | | | |
| Ï | alt U | shift I | | | |
| ï | alt U | I | | | |
| Ñ | alt N | shift N | | | |
| ñ | alt N | N | | | |
| Ó | alt E | shift O | | | |
| ó | alt E | O | | | |
| Ò | alt ~` | shift O | | | |
| ò | alt ~` | O | | | |
| Ô | alt I | shift O | | | |
| ô | alt I | O | | | |
| Ö | alt U | shift O | | | |

## Accents

| | |
|---|---|
| acute ´ | alt E (UK) |
| | Shift alt E (US) |
| breve ˘ | shift alt . |
| circumflex ˜ | shift alt N (UK) |
| | shift alt I (US) |
| dotless ı | shift alt B |
| dieresis (umlaut) ¨ | alt U (UK) |
| | shift alt U (US) |
| macron ¯ | shift alt , |
| overdot ˙ | alt H |
| ring ˚ | alt E (UK) |
| | alt K (US) |
| tilde ˜ | shift alt N (UK) |
| | shift alt M (US) |
| Apple Ó | shift alt H |
| bullet • | alt 8 |
| copyright © | alt G |
| decimal · | shift alt 9 |
| mid point · | shift alt 9 |

## Dipthongs

| | |
|---|---|
| Æ | shift alt ' " |
| æ | alt ' " |
| Œ | shift alt Q |
| œ | alt Q |
| en space | alt space |

## Ligatures

| | |
|---|---|
| fi | shift alt 5 |
| fl | shift alt 6 |
| (Expert set font) | |
| ffi | shift y |
| ffl | shift z |
| ff | shift v |
| eszett | |
| (German long and short s together) ß | alt s |

## Mathematical and other symbols

| | |
|---|---|
| American number symbol # | shift 3 |
| ascii circumflex ˆ | alt I |
| approx/equal ≈ | alt X≈ |
| delta Δ | alt J |
| division ÷ | alt / |
| epsilon Σ | alt W |
| fractions (solidus) / | shift alt 1 |
| (Expert set font) | |
| (= three quarters) | shift I |
| (= two thirds) | shift O |
| (= a quarter) | shift G |
| (= a half) | shift H |
| (= one eighth) | shift J |
| (= three eighths) | shift K |
| (= five eighths) | shift L |
| (= one third) | shift N |
| (= seven eighths) | shift M |
| greater than or equal to ≥ | alt . |
| less than or equal to ≤ | alt , |
| infinity ∞ | alt 5 |
| integral ∫ | alt B |
| logical not ¬ | alt L |
| lozenge ◊ | shift alt V |
| mu μ | alt M |
| not equal to ≠ | alt = |
| omega Ω | alt Z |
| ordinal a ª | alt 9 |
| partial difference ∂ | alt D |
| per thousand ‰ | shift alt R(UK) shift alt E(US) |
| Pi ∏ | shift alt P |
| pi π | alt P |
| plus or minus ± | shift alt = |
| square route √ | alt V |

## Punctuation and other symbols

| | |
|---|---|
| apostrophe ' | shift alt ] |
| dashes | |
| em dash — | shift alt – |
| en dash – | alt – |
| ellipsis … | alt ; |
| guillemets: | |
| (single) ‹ | shift alt 3 |
| (single) › | shift alt 4 |
| (double) « | alt \ |
| (double) » | shift alt \ |
| open Spanish exclamation mark ¡ | alt 1 |
| open Spanish question mark ¿ | shift alt / |
| open Spanish quotation marks ‚ | shift alt 0 |
| quotation marks „ | shift alt w |
| quotation marks: | |
| (single) ' | alt ] |
| (single) ' | shift alt ] |
| quotation marks: | |
| (double) " | alt [ |
| (double) " | shift alt [ |

### Reference marks

| | |
|---|---|
| dagger † | alt t |
| double dagger ‡ | shift alt 7 |
| pilcrow ¶ | alt 7 |
| registration mark ® | alt R |
| section § | alt 6 |
| soft return (gives the option of starting a new line without altering the paragraph format) | shift return |
| temperature ° | shift alt 8 |
| trademark ™ | alt 2 |

## Currencies

| | |
|---|---|
| cent ¢ | alt 4 |
| euro € | shift alt 2 |
| florin ƒ | alt F |
| pound sterling £ | alt 3 |
| yen ¥ | alt Y |

# Appendix 2:
# Paper sizes

## The European ISO system
The standardized ISO stock sizes have three series, A, B and C.

## A series (trimmed)
A sizes are based on a standard sheet, A0. These sizes are used for general printing and stationery.

| | |
|---|---|
| A0 | 841 x 1189mm |
| A1 | 594 x 841mm |
| A2 | 420 x 594mm |
| A3 | 297 x 420mm |
| A4 | 210 x 297mm |
| A5 | 148 x 210mm |
| A6 | 105 x 148mm |
| A7 | 74 x 105mm |
| A8 | 52 x 74mm |

## B and C series
B and C sizes are generally used for large-scale items such as posters and wallcharts.

| | |
|---|---|
| B0 | 1000 x 1414mm |
| B1 | 707 x 1000mm |
| B2 | 500 x 707mm |
| B3 | 353 x 500mm |
| B4 | 250 x 353mm |
| B5 | 176 x 250mm |
| B6 | 125 x 176mm |
| B7 | 88 x 125mm |
| B8 | 62 x 88mm |
| C0 | 917 x 1297mm |
| C1 | 648 x 917mm |
| C2 | 458 x 648mm |
| C3 | 324 x 458mm |
| C4 | 229 x 324mm |
| C5 | 162 x 229mm |
| C6 | 114 x 162mm |

## US standard paper sizes
The United States has four standard sizes.

| | |
|---|---|
| Bond (letterheads, newsletters) | 17 x 22 inches |
| Book (books, catalogues, calendars, annual reports, brochures, magazines) | 25 x 38 inches |
| Text (posters, self-mailers, announcements) | 25 x 38 inches |
| Cover (business cards, annual report covers, greeting cards) | 20 x 26 inches |

## Trimmed page sizes from standard US sheets

| Trimmed page size | No. of pages | No. from sheet | Standard paper size |
|---|---|---|---|
| 3½ x 6¼ inches | 4 | 24 | 28 x 44 inches |
| | 8 | 12 | 28 x 44 inches |
| | 12 | 8 | 28 x 44 inches |
| | 16 | 6 | 28 x 44 inches |
| | 24 | 4 | 28 x 44 inches |
| 4 x 9 inches | 4 | 12 | 25 x 38 inches |
| | 8 | 12 | 38 x 50 inches |
| | 12 | 4 | 25 x 38 inches |
| | 16 | 6 | 38 x 50 inches |
| | 24 | 2 | 25 x 38 inches |
| 4½ x 6 inches | 4 | 16 | 25 x 38 inches |
| | 8 | 8 | 25 x 38 inches |
| | 16 | 4 | 25 x 38 inches |
| | 32 | 2 | 25 x 38 inches |
| 5¼ x 7⅞ inches | 4 | 16 | 32 x 44 inches |
| | 8 | 8 | 32 x 44 inches |
| | 16 | 4 | 32 x 44 inches |
| | 32 | 2 | 32 x 44 inches |
| 6 x 9 inches | 4 | 8 | 25 x 38 inches |
| | 8 | 4 | 25 x 38 inches |
| | 16 | 2 | 25 x 38 inches |
| | 32 | 2 | 38 x 50 inches |
| Oblong | | | |
| 7 x 5½ inches | 4 | 8 | 23 x 29 inches |
| | 8 | 4 | 23 x 29 inches |
| | 16 | 2 | 23 x 29 inches |
| 8½ x 11 inches | 4 | 4 | 23 x 35 inches |
| | 8 | 2 | 23 x 35 inches |
| | 16 | 2 | 35 x 45 inches |
| 9 x 12 inches | 4 | 4 | 23 x 38 inches |
| | 8 | 2 | 23 x 38 inches |
| | 16 | 2 | 38 x 50 inches |

# Further reading
# and resources

## Books

Phil Baines and Andrew Haslam,
*Type & Typography,*
Laurence King Publishing, 2002

Alan Bartram,
*Making Books: Design in British
Publishing since 1945,*
London, British Library,
and New Castle, Del.,
Oak Knoll Press, 1999

Lewis Blackwell,
*Twentieth-Century Type*
(revised edn),
Laurence King Publishing, 2004

Robert Bringhurst,
*The Elements of Typographic Style*
(2nd edn),
Point Roberts, Wash., Hartley &
Marks, 1997

G. V. Carey,
*Mind the Stop:
a Brief Guide to Punctuation
with a Note on Proof-Correction*,
Harmondsworth, Penguin, 1976

Rob Carter, Ben Day
and Philip Meggs,
*Typographic Design: Form and
Communication* (2nd edition),
New York, Van Nostrand Reinhold,
1993

F. Howard Collins,
*Authors' and Printers' Dictionary*
(10th edition),
Oxford University Press, 1969

James Craig,
*Basic Typography:
A Design Manual,*
New York, Watson-Guptill, 1987

Carl Dair,
*Design with Type*,
University of Toronto Press, 1982

Geoffrey Dowding,
*Finer Points in the Spacing and
Arrangement of Type* (revised edn),
Point Roberts, Wash.,
Hartley & Marks, 1995

Eric Gill,
*An Essay on Typography (1931)*,
Boston, Mass.,
David R. Godine, 1988

*Hart's Rules for Compositors and
Readers at the University Press,
Oxford* (39th edition),
Oxford University Press, 1983

Jost Hochuli and Robin Kinross,
*Designing Books:
Practice and Theory*,
London, Hyphen Press, 1996

Richard Hollis,
*Graphic Design: A Concise History*,
London, Thames and Hudson, 1994

John Kane,
*A Type Primer*,
Laurence King Publishing, 2002

David Jury,
*About Face:
Reviving the Rules of Typography*,
Rotovision, 2002

Robin Kinross,
*Modern Typography*,
London, Hyphen Press, 1996

Ellen Lupton and J. Abbot Miller,
*Design/Writing/Research:
Writing on Graphic Design*,
London, Phaidon Press, 1999

Philip Meggs,
*A History of Graphic Design*
(3rd edition),
New York, John A. Wiley & Sons,
1998

Ruari McLean,
*Typographers on Type*,
London, Lund Humphries, 1995

Josef Müller-Brockmann,
*Grid Systems in Graphic Design:
A Visual Communication Manual
for Graphic Designers, Typographers
and Three-Dimensional Designers*,
Niederteufen, Arthur Niggli, 1981

Josef Müller-Brockmann,
*Designer: A Pioneer of Swiss
Graphic Design*, Baden, Lars
Müller, 1995

*The Oxford Writers' Dictionary*,
Oxford, Oxford University Press,
1990

Christopher Perfect and
Gordon Rookledge,
*Rookledge's Classic
International Typefinder*,
revised by Phil Baines and with a
foreword by Adrian Frutiger,
Laurence King Publishing, 2004

Rick Poynor,
*Typography Now*,
London, Booth-Clibborn Editions,
1991

Ben Rosen,
*Type and Typography:*
*The Designer's Type Book*,
New York, Van Nostrand Reinhold,
1963

Adrian Shaughnessy,
'Web Design' in *Eye* magazine, vol.
14, spring 2005, p.37

Herbert Spencer,
*The Visible Word*,
Lund Humphries, 1968

James Sutton and Alan Bartram,
*Typefaces for Books*, London,
British Library, 1990

Jan Tschichold,
*Typographische Gestaltung, 1935;*
*as Asymmetric Typography*,
trans. by Ruari McLean, London,
Faber & Faber, and Toronto, Cooper
& Beaty, 1967

Jan Tschichold,
*The Form of the Book:*
*Essays on the Morality of*
*Good Design*,
London, Lund Humphries, 1991

## Magazines and periodicals

Baseline (UK)

Communication Arts (USA)

Creative Pro (USA)

Creative Review (UK)

Emigre (USA)

Eye (UK)

Fine Print (USA)

Grafik (UK)

Letter Arts Review (USA)

Step-by-Step Graphics (USA)

The Circular (Typographic Circle)
(UK)

Typography Papers (UK)

## Organizations

Association Typographique
Internationale (ATypI)
atypi.org

International Society of
Typographic Designers (ISTD)
istd.org.uk

The Typographic Circle
typocircle.co.uk

Type Directors Club
tdc.org

## Websites of software and type manufacturers

www.planet-typography.com
www.adobe.com
www.agfamonotype.com
www.bertholdtypes.com
www.emigre.com
www.fontshop.com
www.fontsmith.com
www.identifont.com
www.linotype.com
www.microsoft.com/typography
www.pdfzonel.com
www.thefoundrystudio.co.uk
www.typeart.com
www.typeright.org
www.typophile.com
www.unicode.org

# Picture credits

Images not listed below were taken from Erste Hilfe in Typografie by Hans Peter Willberg and Friedrich Forssman, Verlag Hermann Schmidt Mainz, 2000.

*10 left* Letterpress image, Baseline magazine, inside front cover, No.18, 1994; *right, centre* 'Advancing' advertising poster for ING Barings bank, design and art direction: Vince Frost, Frost Design, Sydney; *right, bottom* The Birth Control Book by Howard I. Shapiro, © Penguin 1980, cover design: Lora Starling
*11 left, top* foldout souvenir for riverboat trip on the Thames/Channel Four TV, UK, 1999, design: Kerr Noble; *11 left, second from top* Künstpunkte, poster for arts event, Germany, 2000, design: Nowakteufelknyrim, www.nowakteufelknyrim.de; *11 left, third from top* CBS wall by Louis Dorfman and Herb Lubalin, Central Lettering Record, Central Saint Martins College of Art & Design, London (source of photograph unknown); *11 left, bottom* image by Tomato from their book Mmm Skyscraper I Love You, Booth-Clibborn Editions, 1995; *11 right, top* chapter opener from Catulli et Tibulli, et propertii opera printed by John Baskerville, Birmingham, 1772, Central Saint Martins Museum & Study Collection (photo: Phil Baines); *11 right, centre* Christmas card (280 x 90mm), 1998 'Messianic Prophecies and Matthew's Geneology', Phil Baines Catherine Dixon collection
*15 top,* illustration showing two cases for storing metal type, Central Lettering Record, Central Saint Martins College of Art & Design, London
*20 top,* postcard, FontShop International (FSI), Berlin, Central Lettering Record, Central Saint Martins College of Art & Design, London (photo: Tim Marshall)
*21 bottom,* ice cream wrapper showing the font Lithos (1990) by Carol Twombly, Phil Baines
*78* image of leading from About Face: Reviving the Rules of Typography by David Jury, Rotovision, 2002, page 80
*98 above* Travels in the Land of Kubilai Khan, Marco Polo, © Penguin 2005, cover design: Phil Baines; *98 below,* spread from The Designer and the Grid by Lucienne Roberts and Julia Thrift, Baseline magazine, No. 39, 2002
*99 above left and right,* spreads from Big magazine, design and art direction: Vince Frost, Frost Design, Sydney; *99 below left* The Guardian, 29 September 2005, page 11, © Guardian Newspapers Limited 2005
*118–21* images courtesy Phil Baines Catherine Dixon collection
*152 above* sketchbook made of tracing, graph and cartridge paper, bound in birch, Jayne Knowles; *152 below* hardback stitched book, Baseline magazine, No. 33, 2001
*153 above left* large-format brochure designed by David Jury, Darren Hughes and Kelvin Smith, from About Face: Reviving the Rules of Typography by David Jury, Rotovision, 2002, page 126; *153 above right* The Murder on the Links, Agatha Christie, © Penguin; *153 below left* cover of Nederlandse Postzegels, 1988, design: Irma Boom
*154 above* cover of S,M,L,XL by Rem Koolhaas and Bruce Mau, © 1995 010 Publishers, Rotterdam (www.010publishers.nl); *154 below* hardback book with foil stamping, Baseline magazine, No.23, 1997

# Index